REIKI

A Powerful Catalyst For Personal Transformation and Healing

REIKI

A Powerful Catalyst For Personal Transformation and Healing

A Practical Guide for the Novice, Practitioner, and Reiki Master

with a Collection of Testimonials

Roland Bérard

Disclaimer

This book is not intended as a substitute for the medical advice of physicians. The reader should regularly consult a physician in matters relating to his/her health and particularly with respect to any symptoms that may require diagnosis or medical attention.

Bibliothèque et Archives nationales du Québec and Library and Archives Canada cataloguing in publication

Bérard, Roland, 1950-

Reiki, a powerful catalyst for personal transformation and healing : a practical guide for the novice, practitioner and reiki master with a collection of testimonials

Issued also in French under title : Le reiki, un puissant catalyseur de transformation personnelle et de guérison.

Includes bibliographical references.

ISBN 978-0-9919112-2-6

1. Reiki (Healing system). 2. Mind and body. I. Title.

RZ403.R45B47 2013   615.8'52   C2013-941397-9

Legal deposit - Bibliothèque et Archives Canada 2013
Legal deposit - Bibliothèque et Archives nationales du Québec 2013

Credits

Cover design by KillerCovers

Editing by: June Kallistad - Louise Vandale - Anna Lee-Popham

Reiki symbol image on back cover & title page
©James Kingman/Dreamstime

ISBN : 978-0-9919112-2-6
First publication - August 2013
Roland Bérard

This book is dedicated to the Master within.

It is also dedicated to all those who transform the world, one person at a time, starting with themselves.

CONTENTS

I am not a Healer; I am but a shell,

Spirits work through me and help make people well.

They use me as a channel their Healing Gifts to pour

into the bodies of needy folk, I'm a Channel--nothing more.

Please don't call me a Healer; I'm no different from you,

I just give my time to serve my God and see what I can do.

To help the Spirit Brethren pass on their Healing Balm

and pray that souls I meet each day, experience no harm.

Don't think of me as a Healer, my hands are nothing new,

I'm used just like an instrument to help folk such as you.

And when the time approaches for this earthly frame to die

My Soul will cry out "Thank You God for using such as I."

Author Unknown

INTRODUCTION

Two roads diverged in a wood, and I –
I took the one less traveled by,
And that has made all the difference.

(Frost, 1916, 18-20)

I was introduced to Reiki in 1994. I didn't know anything about energy work but became curious after hearing about it in the naturopath's office where my children were being treated. I decided to take a weekend course on a whim after my fiddle teacher's wife Cecile showed me her Reiki Master's pamphlet and briefly shared her experience of Reiki.

My own experience of this first course was profound. I had always wanted to help others who suffered and this seemed to be a simple way to do it. I was excited and keen to practice on myself as well as family, friends, and anyone else who might be interested in exploring something new. Also, the possibility of treating others from a distance was very intriguing, and I was lucky enough to have the chance to practice it on family members living in another city.

I was impressed to hear that my brother-in-law's shoulder problem, for which he had consulted several practitioners without success, disappeared after one Reiki treatment. My nephew's mononucleosis healed in about a third of the usual time required. These results encouraged me to further my learning.

I never expected to become a teacher. However, three years later, after completing the master level of Reiki, I knew I wanted to share this gift with others. I began to teach.

Reiki was life-changing for me. The self-healing I experienced through Reiki led me to explore personal therapy and pursue other trainings. In 2001, I left full-time work as an engineer and project manager and started a practice so that I could work with people one-on-one and teach.

Reiki was the first healing approach I experienced and learned. After becoming a Reiki Master, I broadened my skills by learning other healing and therapy approaches, such as Barbara Brennan's Healing Science, Emotional Freedom Technique, Theta Healing, Quantum Touch, Hakomi, and recently fasciatherapy (Danis Bois Method) and Core Energetics. I now integrate all these different techniques into my sessions with clients as I facilitate and assist their healing process.

My Reiki practice has evolved into accompanying people on their journey of self-study, growth, and enhanced well-being by integrating energy and consciousness work with body-centered therapies. I have learned to be in a state of loving presence, to follow what wants to emerge in the moment, to trust the organicity of the spontaneous healing process, to have faith that the client already knows what is needed and has the inner resources to heal, and to trust that whatever technique is appropriate will come forth effortlessly as required.

I have grown tremendously in self-awareness and self-love and have been able to help others at a deep level in their own process of transformation. The journey has drastically influenced my relationship with my family, my children, and my intimate partners.

Although it was challenging to change careers and develop a large enough clientele to earn a decent living, I have never looked back. I know now that I am doing my life's work—it is what I came here to do. I am very grateful to my former wife Marla and my two sons Philip and Benoit for their unfailing support and encouragement as we navigated this life change. And I feel very blessed to have learned from many master teachers along the way.

More and more, I am able to live in the present moment instead of letting my past dictate my present experience and become the template for my future. Self-awareness and self-empowerment allow me to make choices in every moment that are more aligned with my True Self.

In writing this book on Reiki, I wish to humbly share my experience and personal approach with novices, practitioners, and masters alike. I have included testimonials received from students and practitioners.

If you are new to Reiki, I hope this book will encourage you to explore this simple, accessible, easy to learn, and life-changing method for yourself to pave the way for your own inner master to emerge. This may enrich what you are already doing or set you in a new direction. Through Reiki, you will learn how to share the gift of who you are with the world, and everyone will benefit. May you offer yourself the truly wonderful gift of Reiki, and may you join countless others whose life has been transformed by Reiki.

If you are a Reiki practitioner you may discover different viewpoints on what you have learned, expand your knowledge, and find useful information to help you in your practice.

If you are a Reiki Master, I hope that this book will offer you alternatives and insights to enhance your teaching material and teaching style.

OVERVIEW

This book is divided into six parts with supporting appendices.

Chapter 1 – **Reiki: What and What For?** presents what Reiki is, its history and guiding principles, and its benefits and uses.

Chapter 2 – **The Energy Field** gives a brief overview of the Universal and Human Energy fields through which Reiki is applied.

Chapter 3 – **Learning Reiki** presents the different levels and what is taught in each one.

Chapter 4 – **Applying Reiki: Guidelines for the Practitioner** presents various aspects of giving treatments that need to be taken into consideration by the practitioner.

Chapter 5 – **Integrating Reiki into your Life and Workplace** presents different ways you can integrate Reiki into your daily life and place of work.

Chapter 6 – **Transformation Through Reiki** talks about the journey of self-awareness and the path of the practitioner from Level 1 to Master.

The appendices offer relevant and complementary material and resources.

CHAPTER 1

REIKI: WHAT AND WHAT FOR?

In this chapter we will explore what Reiki is as well as its history, principles, benefits and various uses.

What is Reiki?

Reiki is a hands-on healing technique that has its origins in Tibet and was "rediscovered" in the late 1800s by Mikao Usui, a Japanese monk who was passionate about healing. Simply put, Reiki is an accessible, easy, and effective way to tap into the potential of universal energy so that you or another can benefit from it.

It is not a sect, nor is it a religion. A Reiki Master is a teacher, not a guru. Reiki is transmitted directly from Reiki Master to student. Students are not pressured to advance to other levels; they are supported by the Reiki Master and encouraged to advance at their own pace, if they so desire.

Although Reiki can be used for others, I stress in my teaching that it is primarily an empowering path unto one's self through alignment to one's true nature and removal of the layers that cover up the master within.

The word Reiki is made up of two Japanese words— Rei and Ki. The "Ki" in Reiki is the vital energy and consciousness that is part of all things, also referred to as Chi, Prana, or Life Force. "Rei" means universal. Together, they mean Universal Energy. This energy is consciousness and unconditional love. When one connects to it and transmits it, it has a calming effect, as it stimulates and supports healing from within. The Reiki energy vibrates a specific frequency close to that of the color violet, which supports healing and conscious awakening.

This simple method of healing is accessible to everyone and is easy to learn in a one- or two-day course. No prerequisites are necessary. Everyone can channel universal healing energy. You will most likely feel its heat when you put a caring hand on someone or when someone puts a caring hand on you. While there are many hands-on healing techniques, Reiki differs from others by its attunements, which increase the capacity to transmit the energy. An attunement is a vibratory transmission performed by the Reiki Master that empowers the receiver.

As simple as it is, taking a Reiki course can be transformative. I continue to teach because of the transformations I witness in my students as they share their experience after having taken a level. Many come back to continue to deepen their experience and knowledge of Reiki. Each level of learning has a cumulative, powerful effect.

Traditional Reiki is learned in three or four levels, depending on the lineage of the Reiki Master. Other forms of Reiki have evolved as additional information, techniques, and symbols have been received by Reiki Masters and integrated into new approaches.

Reiki can be used to treat the self or another person. You do not have to believe in Reiki for it to work for you. You simply have to have an intention for healing. The energy of Reiki cannot do harm, nor can you ever get too much.

Children respond well to Reiki and can be attuned at an early age; they learn and integrate it very quickly. Being attuned early in life is a great advantage in that it allows children to treat themselves and be supported by Reiki to fully develop their potential and share their gifts.

Reiki can also be used on food, water, plants, animals, situations, past and future events, and many other things, as you will discover throughout this book.

A brief history

The Japanese monk Mikao Usui was passionate about healing. Why (in his time and tradition) was it focused on the spiritual rather than the physical aspects of healing? He had probably heard of hands-on healing but did not know enough to practice it, nor could he find anyone to answer his questions.

Usui's curiosity led him on a quest on which he studied everything he could find, including Japanese and Chinese writings and ancient Buddhist texts (known as sutras). It was in one of the sutras from the Tibetan tradition that he found the keys to what he was looking for. During a 21-day fast and meditation on Japan's sacred Mount Kurama, he received the keys to activate and use the symbols that he had found in these ancient texts.

Usui used his discovery to develop a simple and effective hands-on healing method that he named Usui Shiki Ryoho (Usui Healing Method), which he first used to treat poor people in Kyoto's ghetto. He later travelled around Japan to teach those who wanted to learn the method and advance in self-healing and transformation. Usui adopted five principles to "encompass" the method and guide Reiki practitioners. He also recognized the importance of an exchange to ensure maximum benefit for the receiver.

Hawayo Takata, a Japanese-American woman from Hawaii, learned the method after she was treated and healed of tumors in a Reiki clinic set up and directed by Dr. Chijiro Hayashi, who was a student and successor of Usui. Mrs. Takata returned to Hawaii to practice Reiki and later moved to California. In order to make Reiki more acceptable and palatable for the Western mind, she "packaged" what she had learned into three simple, but powerful, courses. By the end of her career in the 1980s, she had trained twenty-two Reiki

Masters. These Reiki Masters have since spread Reiki all over the world.

While the traditional story related in many books on Reiki infers that Dr. Chujiro Hayashi and Hawayo Takata were Usui's only official successors, Usui taught many other Reiki Masters in Japan who continued to practice Reiki. In *The Spirit of Reiki*, (Lübeck et al. 2001) the authors present the results of their research of Usui's other legacies.

Today, Reiki has become popular and is being used professionally as an alternative and complimentary holistic healing approach. It is exciting to welcome young people in their 20s and 30s who are drawn to my Reiki courses.

As the medical profession becomes familiar with its calming and healing benefits, Reiki is being integrated into hospital settings to help patients prepare for and/or recover from medical procedures. I have had the honor of presenting Reiki over the last few years to fourth year medical students at McGill University in Montreal, Canada.

Reiki associations

Reiki is transmitted directly from Reiki Master to student and is not regulated. Most Masters remain loyal to what they have learned from their own Reiki Master while adding a personal touch to their teachings. Although it is not necessary to be a member of an association to practice Reiki professionally, such associations are valuable resources that provide practitioners with credibility and visibility to potential clients.

Typically, associations are made up of Reiki teachers, practitioners, students, and supporting members. They often establish registration requirements and provide teaching guidelines and course material, a code of ethics, member support, resource directories, newsletters, and email groups for members to share their experiences and support each other.

Many of the associations encourage and even organize "Reiki Shares," at which the students, practitioners, and sometimes newcomers to Reiki can share their experiences, meet other practitioners, and exchange treatments with each other. The Share is usually organized by a Reiki Master and provides a forum for practicing and further learning; however, any interested parties can get together and share.

Most associations promote Reiki and assist in setting up programs in communities, health organizations, and hospitals. Some initiate and encourage research studies to validate the results of Reiki.

The original Reiki association formed by Mrs. Takata is called the "American Reiki Association."

Others have followed; listed below are some of the earlier Reiki associations in the USA.

- The Reiki Alliance, formed by Phyllis Lee Furumoto (Hawayo Takata's granddaughter);
- The American International Reiki Association Inc. (AIRA), formed by Dr. Barbara Weber Ray;
- The American Reiki Masters Association (ARMA), formed by Dr. Arthur Robertson, who introduced the four-level system;
- The International Center for Reiki Training, formed by William Rand.

Today, there are associations in many countries. A web search will help you to locate one in your area.

Reiki as a catalyst for personal growth

I stress in my Reiki courses that Reiki is, first and foremost, a path unto the self. This, in my opinion, is one of the most precious gifts of Reiki and the one that never ceases to amaze me.

The attunements transmitted to the student by the Reiki Master during the course increase the level of vibration of the energy field and open up the channel so that the Reiki energy can flow through more easily.

In addition to opening up the energy pathways, the attunements act as a catalyst for personal growth and transformation. They start a process of opening up to the self and aligning with whatever personal or global life task has been chosen for this lifetime. As the integration of the new energies continues, the student may become aware of blocks in the form of limiting beliefs or held emotions that are ready to be released. Opportunities present themselves that were previously outside of awareness. Unexpected synchronicities open new doors congruent with the next step in the life journey.

As the student continues to align with his or her life purpose, life becomes less of a struggle and more nourishing. Attitudes and perceptions of one's life work may change so that it becomes more pleasant or other passions/work more suited to and aligned with the true self may be discovered and followed.

The process leads to people who will assist and support the process, perhaps friends, colleagues, teachers, or therapists. New people and experiences that are aligned with the life task simply begin to show up. The more the student becomes aware of personal dynamics and begins to affect life changes, the more present she or he becomes to the self. More contact with one's self in this way allows for the sharing of each person's true gift and improves relationships.

All this increases the ability to be present and has an impact on the ability to be with those who are treated. Letting go of results and getting the ego self out of the way are other benefits that allow the Reiki energy to flow more easily and more strongly.

Students share many testimonials of this transformation process during successive courses. I am honored to be a witness as they grow, transform, and become happier and more whole.

As I stated in my introduction to this book, Reiki has also influenced me tremendously; it has set me on a path that changed my life and led me to my life's work.

The five founding principles of Reiki

Of the many principles that may guide one's life, Mikao Usui adopted five closely aligned with the teachings of Buddha.

- Just for today, I will not worry.

- Just for today, I will not anger.

- Just for today, I will honor my elders, my teachers, and all living things.

- Just for today, I will earn my living in an honest way.

- Just for today, I will have an attitude of gratitude.

Usui also adopted the principle of exchange for a treatment.

These principles provide a framework for healthy living; integrating them into daily life is a work in progress that continues throughout one's lifetime.

I like the way the principles are formulated. These first three words—JUST FOR TODAY—can easily be adjusted to one's personal situation and capability in the moment "Just for this morning, just for this minute, just for this week or this month."

These few words allow us to integrate the principles at a pace that is in our control and does not require a life-long commitment. We can set our intention and make realistic, achievable, and perhaps even measurable choices in alignment with the principle and our desire to improve our lives and that of those around us.

Reiki Master Barbara, says:

When I first heard the principles I understood the logic behind them. All my life I had tried to take definite decisions in order to change something about myself. My affirmations would always sound something like: "From now on, I will or will not do this or that." When I started applying the principles using the sentence: "Just for today" I began to feel a big weight lifted. I realized that trying to imprint my affirmation in the future would create some stress within me and I usually ended up giving up sooner than I should have in my quest to change.

Integrating the principles and growing with them requires developing the key skill of the Witness or the Observing Self. This skill enables us to watch ourselves with curiosity, non-judgment, and compassion so that we can start to notice our reactions and eventually learn to respond rather than react to what is happening in the moment.

This skill helps us to see how our ego often acts for the wrong reasons. It assists us in developing a mature adult ego that can eventually allow itself to be transcended. Eckhart Tolle (2005) does a wonderful job of helping us to identify and transform the ego in *A New Earth*.

I spend a lot of time during my courses exploring and discussing the principles with my students. I will elaborate on each of them.

Just for today, I will not worry

When we are worried, it is difficult to be present and enjoy what we are doing, those we are with, or what is happening in the moment. Worry always has to do with fear of something unpleasant happening in the future, although it may originate from past experience. We worry about countless things over which we have little or no control: finances, disease, our kids, our work, what others think of us, our self-worth, whether we did the right thing, etc.

Life happens in the moment. The past is over and the future is not yet here; it is but one of countless possibilities. Our past experiences have led us to form beliefs and generalizations about the world. This limits us and prevents us from seeing reality as it is. If we are not aware and not careful, our past can easily become our future. Our beliefs control our thoughts and our way of seeing things. Thus, they control our behavior and the way we organize our present moment experience. If we believe people perceive us in a certain way, we distort how they relate to us and react to them from these distorted views. Their reactions are congruent with our expectations. This is how we create our future based on our past.

It is possible to create a different future once we are aware of this dynamic.

Integrating this principle means: Trust yourself. Trust that you are exactly where you need to be. Trust that life will bring you what you need in order to grow and show you where you need to go. Surrender, not in the sense of giving up but rather giving over to a higher knowing or a higher power.

Eckhart Tolle (2004) expands on the present moment in *The Power of Now* and on how to improve our capacity to live here and now rather than in the past or the future.

"You cannot be yesterday, you can only remember yesterday. You cannot be tomorrow, you can only foresee tomorrow. You can only be in the present." (Desjardins, 2002).

Becoming aware of our behavior makes it possible to change it, and this can sometimes happen in a very short period of time.

Just for today, I will not anger

This is the principle that is challenging for most people, myself included.

When I ask my students: "What do you do with your anger?" here's what they tell me:

- I tend to repress it.
- I express it alone when no one is around.
- I explode. My friends are getting used to it.
- I name it, and it seems to dissolve.
- I don't really get angry.

Our society does not encourage us to allow, express, acknowledge, own, or otherwise deal with anger in healthy and constructive ways. Instead, we are taught to ignore it, repress it, or deny it. The feelings go underground and are usually expressed in a distorted way, often at some unsuspecting and undeserving person. In addition, it gets trapped in the body in the form of tension and/or disease. John Pierrakos, co-founder of BioEnergetics and founder of Core Energetics, used to say that every muscle tension in the body is a place that holds anger.

We may have been hurt by the expression of anger from our parents or other significant adults and authority figures in our lives. When we're young, we cannot know that we are not responsible for another person's anger, and because we are desperately dependent and need to be in relationship with significant adults, we wrongly conclude that we must have been the cause of their anger and that there must be something wrong with us. Then we turn the anger against ourselves.

If we have been hurt by anger or have witnessed violence resulting from anger, we are afraid that if we let our anger out, it will be also destructive and alienate us from others.

Alexander Lowen (1995) defines anger as a survival force that wants to return the organism to wholeness, much like the pressure inside a ball acts to return it to a perfect sphere when a finger is pushed into it (p. 104).

"At the core of all anger is a need that is not being fulfilled. Thus anger can be valuable if we use it as an alarm clock to wake us up—to realize we have a need that isn't being met" (Rosenberg, 1995, p. 104). Rosenberg goes on to show us how we can use this signal to identify the unmet need, express facts in a way that does not blame the other or ourselves, and then make a request for things to change. I strongly recommend his book and the courses that have been created from his method to integrate this extremely important technique into daily life.

This anger signal can be mild or extreme. The progression of the signal can be expressed as follows:

- Annoyance: a mild form of anger, but one that can lead to a build-up of resentment or anger.

- Frustration/Irritation: a slightly stronger signal that can also lead to a build-up of resentment or anger.

- Anger: a much stronger signal, usually controllable.

- Rage: directed at someone with the intention to hurt, but still can be controlled.

- Fury: a very intense and sometimes violent signal, totally out of control.

Although there are times when it may be unjustified or out of proportion, anger can provide the required energy to defend ourselves; to right a wrong; to make sure that our limits have been respected; or even to save a life, including our own. Anger can also be a legitimate and necessary emotion. It is what we do with anger that can be positive or negative. Holding it in is negative and can lead to disease, ultimately cancer. Yet, it can be a "healing emotion" when dealt with in a positive way.

Your anger belongs to you and you alone. You are the only one who can do something about it. Once your anger has been processed and let go, it can no longer cause harm.

So for me, this principle is more about acknowledging, owning, and learning to deal with anger in a constructive way so that our lives, our relationships, and our health can improve and we can be whole and live from our truth.

Just for today, I will honor my elders, my teachers, and all living things

Although this principle may seem straightforward enough, our modern Western society tends to push aside our elders (parents, older persons, retired folks); they are not respected or looked up to for their knowledge and acquired wisdom and are not encouraged to continue to contribute to society.

We squash a spider, an ant, or a mosquito without a second thought.

Few people are aware (and would be disgusted if they were) of how the meat industry shamefully disrespects chickens, pigs, and beef. In order to lower costs, and maximize profits in response to public and shareholders' demands animals destined for food production are given low-grade food and antibiotics and are kept in such cramped quarters that they become aggressive. This aggression is unknowingly transferred to the meat and other products that are then ingested by people who eat them. It is one of the reasons I have stopped eating meat.

Very few people today have had the chance to witness the slaughter of animals as I did when I was young. They cannot begin to imagine the suffering many of these animals endure as they give up their lives for human consumption.

While Native Americans and other Indigenous cultures take the time to give thanks before eating a meal or interacting with nature, such as killing an animal for food or cutting down a tree, this is not taught nor encouraged in our Western society. To some people, it is embarrassing, even on Thanksgiving Day!

We have largely lost respect for Mother Earth. Our forests are being destroyed at an alarming rate, and our waterways and the air are polluted. The genes in our food supply are being modified without sufficient research to ensure there will be no undesirable side effects.

It is time we change our ways before it is too late. Luckily, there are several groups that are aware and working very hard to effect change and to encourage others to live more ecologically, recycle and reuse, reduce consumption, conserve resources, and encourage the move to organic food.

This principle is about being aware of our wastefulness and disrespect for life so that we can make effective change, first in our own attitude, our self-love, and in the way we treat all life. In this way, we make room for gratitude in every moment.

Just for today, I will earn my living in an honest way

Don't lie, cheat, steal, or be dishonest in any way, and charge a fair price for services rendered. This is the first level of this principle.

On a deeper level, it also means living with integrity with ourselves and others. This is not as easy as it sounds. We must first find and listen to our true inner voice. We need to differentiate it from the voices of the super ego, which is comprised of all the internalized voices from society; culture; and authority figures, including parents, teachers, and superiors.

Then we need to learn to follow and speak our truth in our own lives. Many of us were taught to put our needs aside in order to be loved. Saying "NO" and setting limits is very difficult to do when this hasn't been our practice.

We need to learn to live from our passion instead of performing to meet an unattainable, idealized self-image and/or gain approval. We may need to change our work so that it is more in line with what is nourishing. When we do this, we are much happier, which is reflected onto our work environment. We can contribute to our own global vision instead of doing what we think we should to please someone else. Then we can really shine and live the gift of who we are.

I enjoyed my twenty-five years of work as an engineer and project manager, and, although the transition was a real challenge for me and my family, the work I am doing now is so much more nourishing and in alignment with my true nature.

As this principle is integrated, you may begin to question your current work, your friends, and your lifestyle and choose to make some much-needed changes.

Just for today, I will have an attitude of gratitude

Arnaud Desjardins (1998), lifetime seeker and follower of many spiritual leaders, including Swami Prajnanpad, insists in *L'Audace de vivre* that happiness, love, and gratitude are intimately linked (p. 176).

There was a point when I realized that I could be very negative, focusing on what I did not have and what did not work instead of what was there and available. I started keeping a daily journal, and for over a year I wrote down what I was grateful for: simple things like running water in my home, food, a home, friends who love me.

Now I start my day with a series of exercises and meditations, which I finish with "Today I am grateful for," then I name one thing that comes to mind. This sets me up to notice more of what I can be grateful for during the day.

Before every meal I now take the time to bless my food, invoke Reiki energy, give it my own vibration, and give thanks to Mother Earth and all those who helped bring this food to my table. I often take the hand of the person or persons sharing the meal with me and thank them for their presence. This makes these moments sacred as I take the time to enjoy and savor the precious gift of being alive.

As an exercise, take a moment now to become aware of your current state of being. Then, purposefully bring to mind someone or something you are grateful to have in your life. As you get in touch with that, notice the effect on your state of being. Perhaps a good feeling permeates your body and mind, or a smile comes to your lips, or your heart starts to open. Do this simple exercise anytime you notice that you are negative, impatient, worried, or angry.

You can learn to cultivate gratitude for difficult life challenges, such as the loss of a loved one or a serious disease or accident, as you realize that these events have created an opportunity to significantly shift your consciousness and make important life changes in your work and relationships.

Fostering an "Attitude of Gratitude" is life-changing and attracts more and more positive things and abundance into your life.

You can combine this Attitude of Gratitude with saying "YES!" to life, to everything that is happening to you, even the parts that may be difficult. Yes, I take responsibility for having created this in my life. Yes, I trust that there was a reason I did so. Yes, this is not what I want. Yes, I now make a conscious choice to change. And probably the most difficult of all—Yes, I choose to let go of my negativity, and I say yes to being happy.

Do a search on the Internet and subscribe to gratitude reminders or newsletters. You will be glad you did.

The principle of exchange

While the exchange is not listed as one of the five principles of Reiki, Usui began to request something of value in exchange for a treatment after he noticed that some of the people he was helping for free would relapse into their disease state or life struggles.

The exchange plays an important role in the healing journey. It is often not given the importance it deserves but rather is ignored or discounted. Asking for an exchange was a challenging issue for me when I started to give Reiki treatment. I did not feel justified in asking for it until I started to become aware of my beliefs and images around the issue, as well as my own feelings of self-worth.

The exchange rests on the need for balance in the energy of giving and receiving. It is as important for the person giving as it is for the person receiving.

And there may be times when an exchange may not be appropriate.

There are several aspects of this principle that I would like to elaborate on.

Self-responsibility and self-empowerment

You have probably heard the proverb "Give a man a fish and he will eat for a day, teach him how to fish and he will eat for a lifetime." Being a Reiki practitioner, a healing facilitator, therapist, counselor, or helper in any other profession is about empowering others to take control of their lives and create nourishing experiences for themselves. It is not about creating, building, and maintaining a dependent clientele.

We are all 100% responsible for what is happening to us. This is hard to understand for anyone suffering and/or witnessing another's suffering. Taking responsibility is often thought of as accepting blame for what is happening. It really means taking charge of what is happening and being proactive.

In the greater scheme of things, all that happens to us happens for a reason, either because it is part of our life mission or because life is presenting us with an opportunity to grow in consciousness and learn from the experience.

Some people who have had cancer have said that despite the suffering they endured, it was a positive experience. Perhaps they have made significant changes in their lives as a result of their experience or their cancer brought family closer together.

When a person invests in his or her healing journey, they have a much better chance that healing will truly happen and be long-lasting.

The difference between "taking care of" and "caretaking"

"Taking care of" is addressing and catering to needs of someone who cannot help themselves. This help can be short- or long-term depending on the situation, but it is usually limited to doing things that the person is incapable of doing by himself or herself.

"Caretaking," on the other hand, is going beyond taking care. It is taking charge and doing things for the person even when the person is quite capable of doing those things themselves. This may happen out of pity, an inability to be with or accept someone else's suffering, an inability to set limits and say no, a need to feel good about oneself, a need to have someone be dependent on oneself, a desire to honor a cultural tradition, a need to listen to voices of the super ego, a demand to be loved or some other seemingly "good and honorable" reason.

When we're "taking care of" someone, it is helpful and necessary: an act of selfless love. "Caretaking" is more likely an act of selfish love, which actually takes power away from the person who then never learns to be autonomous, take charge, and take responsibility.

As a practitioner, setting a clear intention to be present for the client's highest good is important, as is being aware that unhelpful personal dynamics may be at play.

More on this in a later chapter…

Healthy relationships and clean energy breaks

While you may decide not to request an exchange for one or a few treatments, continuing to do this may have detrimental effects for you and your client or friend.

For the giver/practitioner:

If you continually give to another person without requesting or being offered anything in return, you will likely become resentful because of feeling taken for granted. This may even be unconscious. When this happens and is not named, it will manifest itself in one form or another. You may not be able to be as present, you may be impatient or curt in your interactions, or you may feel obligated and not look forward to future visits. This gets in the way of effective Reiki treatments.

When the person leaves, you may unconsciously "hook" them with an energy streamer that will create an energetic pull on the person.

For the receiver/client:

Some people feel that life owes them something and will want to receive without having to pay. They have not learned to take responsibility. Others share the common belief that a person with a gift of healing has the duty to share it freely anytime it is needed.

The receiver may build up a sense of debt and not know how to deal with it. This will cause resistance to allowing the healing energy to do its work and reduce the potential effect of the treatment.

A fair exchange eliminates these possibilities. Both have contributed and received, there is a clean break in the energy connection. This allows the relationship to remain healthy. The practitioner has no retainer on, or any resentment for, the client. In turn, the client leaves without a debt, without feeling responsible to the practitioner, and without having to take care of the client/therapist relationship.

Recognizing value

As a practitioner, you have invested time and resources in your training, treatment space, and equipment. In addition, you spend time preparing and sharing your gift of Reiki, your presence, and your skills to accompany people on the path of healing. The exchange acknowledges this, as well as your self-worth.

As a client, if you have contributed in some way to the treatment, it means that you value it; you are taking an active part in your own healing journey. Chances are that you will receive more benefits from the treatment that you will be able to appreciate and hold on to.

What to exchange

There are several possibilities. You can exchange anything that is appropriate to the circumstances and is equitable for both parties. Money is a universal unit of exchange; an appropriate price might be an amount comparable to a holistic treatment or massage. Often, people will exchange treatments or agree to exchange services or goods of comparable value.

For a child, it may be a request for a drawing, a small task, or something similar. When I started to practice Reiki, I would treat my seven-year-old son as I put him to bed and he would quickly fall asleep. Our exchange was a hug. This brought consciousness to the principle, and I could see how it impacted our relationship over time.

Family and intimate partners are always doing things for each other, usually in a balanced way. In this case, it is appropriate to simply bring consciousness to the ongoing exchange.

If you are a student and need someone to practice on, the exchange can be the time that the client volunteers so that you can practice.

When is the exchange not required?

There are times when asking for an exchange may not be necessary or appropriate.

If a child is playing and gets hurt and you give Reiki for a short time, a simple smile or thank you may be sufficient.

If you happen to be at the scene of an accident and spontaneously assist someone, you will not pause to ask for an exchange. Whenever I hear or see an ambulance, a police car with lights flashing, or a fire truck go by or if I witness an accident as I am driving along, I send distance Reiki without any thought of exchange.

If a client is not able to pay you for a treatment, you might ask the person to do volunteer work for an equivalent amount of time. While you yourself do not receive anything in exchange for the work you have done, the person will invest in their healing process. This has been well received by clients when I have proposed it. Life will return the favor in kind for you, the practitioner, and you will have gained satisfaction from giving your gift.

I occasionally help people for free if they are in crisis or in difficulty. At other times, I might use a sliding scale and adjust my price to the person's income. This is acceptable to me if I limit it to a small percentage of my clientele.

You may decide to take part in a volunteer program in your community and not ask for an exchange.

Some people (Mother Teresa, John of God, and others) make it their life mission to dedicate their lives to helping others and receive very little or nothing in exchange.

As you integrate this principle, you will be better able to discern whether or not, and how, to apply it.

Dennis, a Reiki practitioner, shares this experience where he deemed that an exchange was not appropriate:

> *I was attending a four-day Mindful Coaching course in North Carolina. One of the participants complained of a bad back whenever we had to move. I did nothing until the last day of the course when, with her permission, I placed my hand on the small of her back. Almost immediately she felt the heat and claimed the pain had disappeared, a pain-free state that lasted for a few days.*

Resistance to giving or receiving

If you are experiencing resistance in asking for an exchange as a practitioner and/or giving as a client, you may need to look at the beliefs and images around this personal dynamic and where exchanges are present or not elsewhere in your life. Getting curious and looking at it in depth with your therapist will yield many benefits in your life.

Benefits and other aspects of Reiki

Reiki is effective on any or all levels: physical, psychic, emotional, and spiritual

When Reiki is received, it acts at whatever level the person is ready to heal in that moment. This means that it can act on any or all of the physical, emotional, psychic, mental, or spiritual levels. The person may or may not experience physical healing. Barbara Brennan (1988), Gary Craig (2008a, 2008b, 2010), and others state that most of our physical ailments have an emotional root. Releasing on the emotional level may eventually lead to healing on the physical, mental, psychic, or spiritual levels.

When healing does not occur on the physical level, Reiki may help to ease the transition at the end of life.

Reiki is a holistic healing method that is simple and pleasant

What can be simpler than just being there and placing your hands on someone? In Reiki, all we have to do is hold a clear intention to be present and available for Reiki energy to flow through and then put our hands on or just above the areas to be treated. Nothing else is required. The energy flows and does the rest. Hard to believe, isn't it? Often the client becomes relaxed to the point of falling asleep and gets up feeling wonderful at the end of the treatment.

Reiki adapts itself to the needs of the receiver

Giving a Reiki treatment is the offer of a healing template. The person does the rest. The energy being administered on one area of the body will flow elsewhere as required through the energy meridians, which are the channels that distribute the energy throughout the body.

Reiki may energize the body and soul

A person will usually feel more energized after a Reiki session. They will relate more harmoniously with others, although, in some cases, the expression of their emotions may be surprisingly intense at first as the healing integration sets in.

As the Reiki energy comes through, the practitioner also benefits from the energy. I often feel better at the end of my day's work than I did when I started.

Reiki regulates the energy system

The human energy field, often referred to as the aura, is comprised of energy centers (called chakras, a Sanskrit term meaning "wheel") and energy bodies. When disease, or dis-ease, sets in, the energy centers or energy channels in the body become clogged and the flow of energy stagnates or ceases altogether. As the Reiki energy circulates through the body and energy centers, these may clear, thus allowing the energy to flow more freely. In this way, the energy system may be regulated with Reiki.

Reiki can dissolve blocks and enhance total relaxation

Blocks are places where the energy is held and does not flow. This is usually felt as a tension or discomfort somewhere in the body—a lump in your throat, muscle tension, a sickly feeling in your gut. As Reiki is taken in, it dissolves these blocks, freeing the energy flow and relaxing the body.

Reiki encourages the elimination of toxins

As tensions dissolve and stagnant energy clears, toxins held in these areas will be released and eliminated by the body through respiration, sweat, urination, or bowel movements. Drinking water after a session and in the days that follow will help to move and release the toxins.

Reiki may re-establish physical wholeness and spiritual health

This is likely to happen over a series of Reiki treatments as the energy field becomes more balanced and the person integrates the healing on all levels.

Reiki reinforces and accelerates the natural process of healing

Reiki is complementary and supports any other healing approach or therapy and may result in:

- Reduced pain and inflammation;
- Accelerated healing from wounds, fractures, and surgery;
- Accelerated coagulation of blood from open wounds;
- Reduced pain and inflammation and perhaps decreased need for medication and painkillers;
- Reduced side effects from chemo and radiation. Radiation treatments burn the skin and underlying tissue. When Reiki is applied, there will be less pain and the skin will regenerate more quickly. Side effects from chemotherapy such as nausea, indigestion, and fatigue will be less pronounced or altogether eliminated.

Complete cure at times

As was the case with Hawayo Takata, Reiki may bring on a cure of the condition being treated without any medical intervention. However, a complete cure can never be assured through Reiki; the practitioner is not in control of the client's healing process and should not make any promises or suggestions of a complete cure. A Reiki practitioner does not diagnose medical conditions and will always recommend that a client consult a health professional for any condition.

Facilitates peaceful death

At other times, Reiki will facilitate a smoother transition from the combined effects of presence, relaxation, reduced pain, emotional release, and spiritual development.

I worked with a cancer patient for a few weeks, and just as I arrived for a treatment, he passed away. The work we did leading up to that time helped him prepare for end of life, and his wife had definitely noticed the effect. He appreciated my presence, and I got the impression that he had waited for me to be there before passing so that his wife would not be alone in that moment. I stayed until a family member was able to come to be with her.

Uses for Reiki

Your imagination is the only limit to the uses of Reiki. Try it on anything. "Just do it! Do Reiki, Reiki, Reiki, and then you shall know!" was a phrase that was constantly repeated by Mrs. Takata (Haberly, 1990, p. 49).

Here are some of the ways Reiki can be applied:

Self-treatment

What a gift to be able to use Reiki for self-healing! Applied on a consistent basis, that is, every day or as often as possible, it can help keep your energy field balanced and improve and maintain your physical and emotional health, as well as your relationship to yourself and others. Over the long term, applying Reiki consistently will improve your life experience.

When applied to an injury, Reiki will help to reduce pain and swelling and accelerate blood clotting. On a recent trekking expedition, I developed painful blisters on my feet. After working on them with Reiki overnight, I was able to continue walking the next day without undue pain even though I lost two toenails in the process.

You can apply it when you are stressed out by simply putting your hands on the area of the body you are drawn to. Just before an important meeting, applying Reiki will calm and center you. If you are experiencing a strong emotion, such as anger or anxiety, it will also help.

You can use it to fall asleep faster or simply to relax. Simply put your hands on the area of concern or, if you have more time, on all the main energy centers and joints (see Appendix A). Let your intuition guide you to the areas of your body and/or the energy field that needs attention.

During pregnancy

Reiki is useful during pregnancy to deeply connect to and treat the fetus as it grows to maturity. This will have a calming effect on the mother and the child. The Reiki can be self-administered or received by another.

Alison, a Reiki practitioner from Montreal, writes:

I gave a lot of Reiki to my baby while she was in my womb. It was a way to connect with her and relax myself. I am sure that it helped me and that she felt it.

Treating your inner child

As we grow up and learn about and interact with the world around us, we have many positive experiences that guide us and help us mature into capable and responsible adults. We also experience trauma from which we create generalizations and limiting beliefs about the world. Parts of our psyche get frozen in time from these events and we continue to experience the world from these wounded places whenever circumstances or people remind us of those situations.

We sometimes refer to this young place inside us as the Inner Child. The Inner Child has been stunted in its exuberance and wonderment of the world and cannot (dares not) experience life in a spontaneous and joyful way. The stirrings of the Inner Child are discounted or even ignored by his or her wounded adult. He or she needs love and attention in order to grow in those places where it got stuck.

You can send Reiki to your Inner Child to help it become whole and experience pleasure in all aspects of life.

Treating traumatic events in your life

In the same way that you can send Reiki to the Inner Child, you can send it to traumatic events in your past. Reiki energy will act on your past self and past circumstances to help release any trapped emotions from the event.

Catherine, a Reiki practitioner, shares her experience of treating trauma in her life:

> *One day I was using Reiki on a trauma of mine related to the abandonment I experienced as a baby. I have brothers and sisters who also experienced the same abandonment issue. While I was doing the treatment, [I was] visualizing the past and was wrapping myself as a baby with healing energy, the souls of my brothers, sisters and parents appeared. I could feel their trauma even though they had never talked about it in real life. During the treatment, the universal energy surrounded us all and I suddenly realized that my whole family had experienced suffering whereas I had only focused on my own.*

Fears and phobias

You can treat both of these in the same way that you treat situations. Imagine your fears and phobias between your hands and send Reiki as long and as often as needed. If you have taken level 2, you can invoke the symbols to further empower the treatment.

Treatment of others: friends, family, and clients

You will be surprised at the effectiveness and impact on those you treat, even immediately after having taken the course. Almost all my students are amazed at their experience during the course. Many relax to the point of falling asleep

Many of my students have reported that their pet dog or cat would come into the room and lie under the table when they were giving a treatment or come sit on their lap if they were treating themselves. Some have noticed a change in the behavior of their dog or cat immediately after coming home from the first evening of the Reiki course.

Another of my students was delighted to get a job in an equestrian center where treating the horses with Reiki was one of her principle tasks.

When our turtle would get agitated and claw relentlessly at the corner of his aquarium, he would usually calm down when I put my hands just outside the aquarium to beam Reiki to him.

Plants

Kirlian photography demonstrates and confirms that plants also have an energy field (Brennan, 1988, p. 39). Plants and gardens respond well to Reiki. Bernard Grad of McGill University in Montreal performed controlled experiments on seeds in the 1970s and demonstrated accelerated growth in response to the energy from a healer's hands.

Several of my students have also reported that their houseplants flourished and improved after receiving Reiki.

Clearing and charging crystals

Crystals and gemstones are often placed in a room to purify the space or are worn on the body as clearing agents. They accumulate the stagnant energy. Reiki can be used to clear and recharge crystals and gemstones by simply holding them and applying Reiki.

Home and work environment

You can positively influence your home or work environment with Reiki. Simply imagine and hold the office or work environment in your hands and intend Reiki. Or, you can send Reiki to the workplace with your palms out towards the different areas of the space. If you are working on a project or a file, simply hold it between your hands and intend Reiki. Reiki will act on the collective energy of those involved to bring harmony. The results will be in the direction of everyone's highest good and might be different than what you had envisioned.

Mother Earth

Send Reiki to Mother Earth by imagining her between your hands and intending Reiki.

Situations or world events

Reiki will also affect any situation that you treat. This could be a relationship issue, a conflict, a world event, political strife, or any other situation that is not harmonious and could use a helping hand. Again, this will act on the collective energies of all those involved for their highest good. I make it a daily practice to send Reiki to family, friends, clients, and world situations.

Abundance

Reiki can work to bring abundance into your life. This can take any form—love, money, work, or whatever else you need.

Past and future events

The time and space barrier dissolves when working with energy, so you can treat past events and future situations.

When I worked as a project manager, I would send Reiki ahead to upcoming meetings, especially when visiting a challenging client. The meetings went more smoothly than I would have imagined. The participants seemed more aligned with the common goals and there was less confrontation during the discussions.

Whenever I have a therapy session, a massage, or other type of self-care activity, I send Reiki ahead so that my Higher Self and that of the practitioner or therapist can be guided during the session.

Other creative uses: car, computer, etc.

One of my students related how the Check Engine indicator light on her car disappeared after she sent it Reiki. While this may seem unlikely or preposterous, remember that all matter is energy and has consciousness, and consciousness responds to energy. Loving your car in this way will help to make it last longer and serve you better.

Try it on anything!

Be creative, try it out on anything, and let yourself be surprised by the results.

<u>Cautionary measures</u>

Diabetes

Diabetics who monitor their blood sugar levels on a regular basis need to be aware that Reiki is very likely to lower the blood sugar level during or after a treatment. Remember to check it after the treatment to ensure proper follow-up.

High blood pressure

Those suffering from high blood pressure should be aware that Reiki is likely to lower the blood pressure. It should be monitored after a treatment. The client's medical professional should be advised and consulted as required.

<u>Limits of Reiki</u>

The above benefits may make Reiki seem magical, but it is not a cure-all.

Reiki works on the many levels and can have surprising results. However, it is a complimentary approach that supports other work. A Reiki practitioner cannot and does not diagnose medical conditions. Always consult a medical professional for any health related issues.

Clients will very likely notice benefits in the short- and medium-term and are advised to keep their health professionals informed about their progress so that any medications can be adjusted as necessary.

Summary of Chapter 1

Reiki has its origins in Tibet and was rediscovered towards the end of the 19th century by the Japanese monk Mikao Usui. It is a simple, effective, and accessible method of hands-on healing that also acts as a catalyst for personal transformation and a deeper connection to oneself and to one's mission in life.

The following five basic principles guide the Reiki practitioner:

- Just for today, I will not worry;

- Just for today, I will not anger;

- Just for today, I will honor my elders, my teachers, and all living things;

- Just for today, I will earn my living in an honest way;

- Just for today, I will have an attitude of gratitude.

The additional principle of exchange ensures the participation of the receiver in his or her healing journey as well as equity between the giver and the receiver.

The Reiki energy is channeled by the practitioner and is offered as a healing template to the receiver, who takes it in at her or his own rhythm. Healing can take place on any level, physical, emotional, mental, psychic, or spiritual. Reiki has many benefits, from simple relaxation to accelerated healing. It can also facilitate an easier death should that be the soul's journey.

Reiki can be used for oneself, other people, animals, plants, food, objects, and situations. It can be transmitted at a distance and can act on the past, the present, and the future.

It must be remembered that Reiki is a complement to conventional medicine and that it does not guarantee a cure or healing. The Reiki practitioner does not diagnose medical conditions and does not prescribe medication. This remains within the domain of medical professionals.

CHAPTER 2

THE ENERGY FIELD

Reiki acts through the energy field (the aura) to affect the physical, emotional, mental, psychological, or spiritual aspects of the person being treated. This chapter will give a brief overview of the energy field, describe energy blocks, and show how the field can be sensed with the hands or seen with the eyes.

The field and chakras

The field

The universal energy field is made up of energy that permeates the Universe and interconnects all things. It has commonly been referred to as Vital Energy, Chi, Ki, or Prana. This energy has consciousness and nurtures all living things and all matter. Brennan (1993, pp. 13-30) lists a comprehensive history of references to, and measurements of, the universal energy field in *Light Emerging*.

Barbara Brennan (1988, p. 41) defines the aura as that part of the universal energy field that is intimately connected to human life, including the body. The aura is made up of chakras (energy centers) and levels (commonly referred to as energy or etheric bodies). This energy field is a template for the physical body and a vehicle for all psychosomatic reactions in that the aura defines our personality and how we interact with others in relationships and groups.

The chakras

Chakra is the Sanskrit word for "wheel." Chakras act as funnels, which spin and "collect" the energy from the universal energy field and metabolize it for use by our body. This energy is distributed throughout the body to nourish the endocrine glands and specific organs and body parts. Each chakra also governs a psychodynamic function as well as being a receptor of information. As an example, the fifth chakra nourishes the vocal and respiratory apparatus and the esophagus. Psycho-dynamically, this chakra governs our capacity to receive, ask for what we need, and express ourselves to others and in society. It is the receptor through which we perceive sound, taste, and smell.

There are seven main chakras and many other secondary chakras. The locations of the seven main chakras correspond closely to that of the endocrine glands. There is a chakra located at the head (crown chakra); another at the perineum (root chakra); and five others located at the third eye (forehead), throat, heart, solar plexus, and pelvis (sacrum). Each of the five latter chakras has a front and a rear aspect. In general, the head chakras govern our reason; the front aspects of the throat, heart, solar plexus and sacral chakras govern our emotions; and their rear aspects along with the root chakra govern our will and our capacity to manifest.

A healthy chakra spins clockwise (according to Barbara Brennan (1988, p. 71), although some other traditions indicate that they alternate between clockwise and counter-clockwise) and draws energy from the universal field to nourish the body and relate in healthy ways with our environment.

"When the chakras are functioning normally, each will be 'open', spinning clockwise to metabolize the particular energies needed from the universal field... When the chakra spins counterclockwise, the current is flowing outward from the body, thus interfering with metabolism. In other words, the energies that are needed and that we experience as psychological reality are not flowing into the chakra when it is spinning counterclockwise. We thus label the chakra as 'closed' to incoming energies". (Brennan 1988, p. 71)

An unhealthy chakra is either undercharged and takes in little or no energy or is overused/abused and leaks out or pushes energy away. The unhealthy chakra distorts the energy and does not nourish the body and spirit in a healthy way.

John Pierrakos (1990) says that when a chakra is open, the life experience in this area of life is positive and nourishing, but that if it is closed, the experience is not nourishing,, but challenging.

As an example, if your throat chakra is open, you will be able to ask for what you need and freely express yourself. Therefore, your experience in communication will be positive and nourishing. However, if your fifth chakra is closed, you will refrain from expressing and will not feel understood and, of course, will not feel heard. This will lead to frustration and an eventual closing off or a feeling of isolation and aloneness.

The Sevenfold Journey (Judith, 1993) and *Eastern Mind/Western Body* (Judith, 2004) do an excellent and very thorough job of describing what is associated with each chakra and how the chakra can be healthy, overused, or deficient. Anodea Judith describes ways of returning each chakra to wholeness. She shows how the chakra system is a two-way system—manifesting from the spiritual to the material and, vice versa, from the material to the spiritual.

The energy or etheric bodies (the aura)

According to Barbara Brennan (1988), the Human Energy Field has seven levels that each vibrate at a unique frequency. Each level is a complete "body" that radiates out from the core and "sits" just above the physical body and the other levels in correspondingly higher levels of vibration (they are not layered like an onion). Some of the bodies are actually very fine grids of lines of light, which are the template for the cells to align and grow in the physical body.

The complete aura usually radiates out approximately three and a half feet from the body, more or less, depending on a person's physical or emotional state. In countries where there is high population density, the aura may be smaller, as personal space is compressed.

The first three levels relate to our personality aspects (physical sensations, emotions with respect to self, and mental or rational mind). The fourth level relates to our relationships with others and is the bridge between our personality and our spiritual aspects. Levels five, six, and seven relate to our spiritual aspects (divine will, divine love, and divine mind).

In the same way that a magnetic field influences its surroundings, the human aura also affects its environment.

The Subtle Body (Dale, 2009) presents the many different theories on energy fields and chakras.

Blocks in the field

Energy taken in by the chakras from the universal field is metabolized for use by the human body. The energy is distributed throughout the body by energy points called nadis and energy pathways called meridians. You are probably familiar with these terms if you have had acupuncture treatments.

Ideally, the chakras would freely take in energy and distribute it unhindered to all parts of the body. However, when we are stressed or injured, the chakras or energy meridians might get clogged or damaged and the energy may accumulate and stagnate in certain areas. Wherever there is a muscle tension, there is blocked energy, usually accompanied by a held emotion. The block may be temporary and released once the stress has passed, but often the stress cannot be released for many different reasons; it becomes chronic and the area remains blocked. Thus, the parts of the body that need energy cannot get it or accumulate too much. This eventually leads to disease.

Reiki energy works by acting on the energy field to release stagnant or blocked energy. Since all disease and disease show up and begin in the aura, healing can be addressed directly through it. Once the energy field is cleaned and realigned, this cascades down into the physical dimension to promote healing on all levels: physical, emotional, mental, psychic, or spiritual.

When a person is receiving a Reiki treatment, it is very common for the person to relax. Often the body releases stress in small spasms and emotions may be felt and released.

Sensing and perceiving the field

You can sense the field kinesthetically (physically) or see it visually by using these two simple exercises.

Sensing

You can sense the energy field by putting your hands any distance apart and then bringing your consciousness to the palms of your hands. Then, just as you intend or start to move your hands together, you may notice a sensation between your hands—pressure, resistance, temperature (often hot, but could be cold), tingling, density, or form. If you do not feel anything, keep bringing your conscious awareness to your palms and persist.

Seeing

If you put up your hands with fingers spread against a white or dark surface and then look with a soft focus, you may be able to discern a soft hue of light blue or grey pulsating around your fingers. You may be able to see this hue or even see colors when a person is sitting against such a background. I sometimes see this when watching a speaker at a conference. In wintertime, it is easy for me to see the energy field of trees and shrubs against a snowy background.

Summary of Chapter 2

The Reiki energy is transmitted through the energy field. It enters the practitioner's crown chakra and is directed to the heart and then through the palms of the hands. The client takes it in through his energy field by way of the major joints and major energy centers called chakras. These are the places where the energy penetrates most easily into the field.

We can, however, lay the hands on any area of the body that needs it, such as a wound or any area that is in pain or diseased.

The energy field, often referred to as the aura, is composed of the chakras and the energy bodies, which are the template upon which the physical body cells grow. Disease or dis-ease are present in the energy field in the form of blocks, distortions, and stagnant energy. We can therefore treat by way of the energy field. A Reiki treatment can help to harmonize and balance the energy field, and this presents an opportunity to return to equilibrium on all levels—physical, emotional, mental, psychic, and spiritual.

It is possible to learn to perceive the energy field.

CHAPTER 3

LEARNING REIKI

After reading this far, you are probably curious about learning Reiki. This chapter presents the different levels of learning and the course content.

How Reiki differs from other hands-on healing methods

There are several aspects of Reiki that differentiate it from other hands-on healing approaches, such as Healing Touch, Quantum Touch, Therapeutic Touch, Reconnective Healing, EMF Balancing (Electromagnetic Field Balancing), Brennan Healing Science, and others.

One of these aspects is its simplicity. In Reiki, all that is required is for the practitioner to be present as a channel to make the healing energy available to the client. Once the basic hand positions are learned, all one has to do is lay the hands on the various energy centers and major joints and the Reiki does the rest. No other techniques are taught to work on the energy field. The energy is not directed in any way; the practitioner is in "allow" mode, which means that only the energy needed by the client comes through and goes where it needs to go.

Another important difference is the attunement, which is a powerful initiation ritual that is transmitted from Reiki Master to student. The attunement opens up the energy field and increases the capacity to run energy for the client. This energetic transmission, as explained elsewhere, is also a catalyst for personal growth and transformation.

A third difference is the various symbols that deepen the connection between practitioner and client and amplify the amount and/or intensity of the energy transmitted and the resultant healing effect.

The Reiki course also gives a basic framework for the practitioner to create a safe and sacred healing container for the client, an important aspect that, in my experience, is often neglected by some of the other approaches that only teach techniques.

Learning the method

Most of my first level students have never experienced Reiki or energy. They come because they are curious about it or perhaps because a friend has recommended Reiki to them. Others have received Reiki or similar treatments before and want to learn how to treat themselves and others. Still others have discovered that they have a "gift" of healing and want to find out more about it and how best to use it. Many are not comfortable talking about their experience to friends, family, and co-workers for fear of being misunderstood or ridiculed.

All participants discover a wonderful and simple system of self-healing. They are really happy to be able to share the experience with like-minded individuals with whom they can continue to exchange. Many are touched by the loving energy they feel during the course and just how simple it can be to be present with someone in a loving, effortless, and healing way.

If you are drawn to learn Reiki, you must first decide with whom you will take the training. In Appendix B, you will find suggested questions to ask that can help you narrow your search and find someone who will inspire you, whom you will trust, and with whom you will feel comfortable. You may decide to meet and perhaps get a treatment from this Master to help you make your decision.

Traditional Reiki systems

As stated earlier in the brief history of Reiki, Mrs. Takata condensed what she had learned in Japan into three levels, from novice to Reiki Master/Teacher. A Reiki Master who has taken these three levels can then initiate students to all the levels.

Dr. Arthur Robertson, who was initiated as a Reiki Master by Iris Ishikuro, a friend and student of Mrs. Takata, took the initiative to split the third/master level into two separate levels in order to give the Reiki Master more time to integrate the teachings. He also added a new symbol (breath of the fire dragon), positions in which to hold the hands (kanjis), and an initiation ritual to this fourth level, which he called Raku-Kei Reiki. Students initiated in this lineage complete four levels to become a Master/Teacher: One, Two, Three, and Master/Teacher. Originally, this lineage allowed third level students to initiate and teach the first two levels. Recently, however, at least in my lineage, this has been discontinued so that the level 1 and 2 students can fully benefit from all that has been integrated in the four levels by the Reiki Master/Teacher. I fully agree with this approach.

While it may appear contradictory, both of these systems are currently recognized as Traditional Usui Reiki as far as I am able to determine. The first two levels teach the same material.

Extensions and expansions of Reiki

Many variations have evolved from the traditional Reiki system. Reiki Masters who received new information and symbols, or otherwise changed and/or added to the traditional systems, have given it a new name. Some that I am aware of are Reiki Plus, Lightarian Reiki, and Karuna Reiki. The book *Le Reiki Aujourd'hui: De l'origine aux pratiques actuelles (Reiki Today: From its Origin to Current Practice)*

(Mary, 2005) gives a comprehensive list and a brief description of many of these expanded systems. At the time of this writing, it has not yet been translated into English.

Preparing for a Reiki initiation

The following guidelines will help you to prepare for a Reiki course in order to enhance your absorption of the teachings and the energies transmitted during the course.

If you are using psychotropic drugs (anti-depressant) medication, discuss this with your Reiki Master to see if taking a Reiki course is appropriate for you at this time.

For the three days prior:

- Reduce or eliminate the intake of any stimulants, such as sugar, coffee, alcohol, and drugs;
- Eat light meals and reduce or eliminate meat, which requires a lot of energy to digest;
- Rest and take time to reflect on your life and see what may need transforming or reorienting;
- Abstain from sexual activity to keep your sexual energy;
- Plan quiet evenings during and immediately after the course.

For the next few of days after the course, if possible:

- Continue to enjoy quiet time and rest;
- Stay away from violent movies or the news;
- Put off important decisions as you will be in an expanded state of consciousness;
- Make love;
- Read a good book;

- Avoid unhealthy relationships;
- If you work out, take care not to overdo it as you may feel really energized;
- Give yourself a Reiki treatment every day.

The teachings

Because each level of initiation is a powerful catalyst for personal growth, the students are given ample opportunity to reflect on why they have come and what it is they might want to transform in their lives. Each initiation ritual is an opportunity to meditate and receive guidance and clarity.

In all the levels, I invite the presence of Usui, Hayashi, and Takata, all other ascended masters, Guides, Angels as well as the Ancestors. Together with their presence and the students' Higher Selves, we create a sacred, safe, and loving container for sharing, growth, and insight.

In each of the levels, I time is allowed to practice what is learned. Ample time is available to share experiences and answer questions.

I suggest two to three months between levels 1 and 2, three to six months between levels 2 and 3, and six to eight months between level 3 and the Master/Teacher level. The process will take one and a half to two years of learning, integrating, and practicing the art.

It is not required to take all the levels from the same Reiki Master. Most Reiki Masters will recognize each other's teachings. It can be advantageous to learn from different teaching styles. I took all my levels from one Reiki Master, but did the master level with another to round out my training experience.

While it is possible with some Reiki Masters to learn all the levels in one or a few weekends close together, this is a huge mistake and not recommended. This short time will not allow you to integrate the energies, the teachings, and the techniques of one level before moving on to the next one. You will likely then teach from the mental and not from the heart, and the teaching will not be supported by experience.

Individual or group class

Even though some students request individual initiations, learning Reiki in a group is preferred because the group setting creates a powerful energy container in which the students can benefit from the sharing of others and exchange practice treatments while the Reiki Master is available to provide assistance and guidance. I only teach individually if circumstances absolutely require it.

Level 1

Claudia, a Reiki student, explains her experience of Reiki Level 1:

> *I wanted to thank you again for our Reiki course on Monday; I feel like a new person. I was in a bad mood Monday night and Tuesday morning, but then Tuesday afternoon, it was like a weight was lifted and I've been feeling more confident, not scared to be who I really am. If someone says something that bothers me, I don't keep it inside anymore. I dance more, I laugh more, and I love myself more. (I cried a bit too but it didn't last long—all part of the transformation.) I took out a picture of myself as a child and said, "Look how cute I was!" I'd been beating myself up for years; now I don't feel self-critical, I've stopped that and I'm not looking to be perfect anymore! This all happened since Monday! I can't help but feel excited; I'm so thankful. I feel that I will continue to grow by leaps and bounds. I am doing*

Reiki on myself everyday, as was suggested, and I feel the effects everyday.

Level 1 is an introduction to Reiki and energy work and is generally taught in two days, although there are some Reiki Masters who teach it one day. Personally, I prefer to teach it over two days because I believe that the students can better integrate the teachings and energies received when given the extra time during the night. This also allows the students to reflect and ask questions the next day.

In this level, the students learn the history of Reiki, what it is, its benefits, how it works, and what it means to channel energy for oneself and another. The principles are also introduced and discussed.

The students are then taught how Reiki can be used for self-treatment. In most lineages, the students are taught how to treat another person individually and in a group. (I am aware that some Reiki Masters prefer to limit level 1 to treating the self and only teach how to treat another in the level 2.)

The students learn how to prepare for a treatment so it can be most effective, as well as what might get in the way of a treatment and when it might not be appropriate to give Reiki. Some teachers, depending on their level of knowledge, may teach aspects of the energy field and chakras and some may teach the students how to ground. Grounding, as will be explained later, allows the practitioner to tap into the Earth's low energy vibration, and which greatly increases the power and effectiveness of the treatment.

The students are given time during the course to do a full self-treatment and practice giving and receiving a treatment with another person and with a group.

During the first level, the students each receive four separate attunements (also referred to as initiations) from the Reiki Master. While everyone has the capacity to transmit universal energy through the hands, the sacred mantras and symbols used during the ritual have the effect of raising the level of vibration and opening up the energy pathways. This greatly increases each student's capacity to receive and transmit the Reiki energy. The four attunements are cumulative and the fourth one "seals" the process.

Each person experiences the attunement in the way that is appropriate for him or her; there is no right or wrong way. Some have a profound emotional or spiritual experience, while others feel almost nothing. Whatever the experience, there is no doubt that the energies are transmitted and are effective. The results may be experienced at a later time in whatever way is appropriate for the student.

I usually lead an exercise at the beginning and end of the class so that the students can compare their capacity to run and feel the energy in their hands. Many are amazed at the heat they feel from their hands or those of their classmates, and many experience a lot of heat throughout the body as they are giving their first treatments. It is always fun to witness their amazement and the enthusiasm as students share their experience.

The capacity to receive the Reiki energy is permanent and will always be available, regardless of how long one goes without using it. It is simply necessary to intend it and it flows.

Pamela, a student, relates her experience of level 1:

My life has moved significantly since attending Reiki level 1 training a couple of years ago. I was quite overwhelmed with the initiation and physically, emotionally, and mentally felt an "opening" occurring in an instant, so much so that there were brief, intense, and sudden tears. I was, in fact, a little stunned by the power of the experience and later at home it took some time to integrate.

I have since used what I have learned with my family and, significantly later, with my dog. Within a year of taking Reiki 1, I discovered a passion for and pursued certification training in animal assisted therapy, also known as zootherapy. I completed my studies and obtained a diploma in the spring of 2011. My magical golden retriever, an SPCA dog named April, found her way to me through an undeniable series of synchronistic events. She is my working partner, and I regularly use Reiki on her. The results on her are more visible to me then when I have occasion to perform it on humans.

I think the Reiki 1 initiation for me was no accident; I was drawn to it and ready for the heart opening changes it would bring. It seems quite natural now when I look back on the progression of events. I hope to continue further in Reiki, as it is very complementary to my new profession. Blessings to you, Roland, for helping me get here.

Level 2

In the second level of Reiki, the student learns three sacred symbols that greatly increase the power of the treatments. The student also learns to send Reiki from a distance, which opens up the possibility of treating anywhere on Earth, or in the Universe for that matter. In addition, a new technique called Mental/Emotional Reiki is taught.

The students are invited to share their experiences of the first level and the principles and any aspects of level 1 that may be unclear are reviewed.

The Reiki Master transmits two attunements that further increase the vibratory level of the energy field and the capacity to receive and transmit the energy. This second level is a further catalyst for personal growth and alignment with the life task.

Time is allowed to practice giving a treatment using the new symbols with the standard positions, the new Mental/Emotional technique, and the distance treatment.

Level 2 symbols

The Reiki symbols each act in different ways to increase the effectiveness of the treatments. They are activated when their sacred geometry, color, and name are combined in a specific way. The symbols are not effective if a person has not been initiated into Reiki by a Reiki Master.

Although the images of the Reiki symbols have been published by some authors and can be found on the Internet, Reiki students are asked to keep them confidential in order to respect their sacred nature. Here is a brief overview of each one.

The distance symbol

This first symbol creates and maintains an etheric (energetic) connection between the sender and receiver during a distance treatment. It is a symbol that encompasses the complete holistic treatment. Its general meaning is that "the Light/Divine/Buddha/Master in me recognized the Light/Divine/Buddha/Master in you." It is a symbol that fosters humility and equality, reminding the sender that we are all equal and that everyone's healing journey is unique and not to be judged.

The power symbol

This second symbol increases the power of energy where it is applied and helps to remove blocks and free stagnant energy. This symbol can also be used outside of treatments for food and water and to clear objects (such as crystals), rooms, and spaces of stagnant undesirable energy.

The mental/emotional symbol

The third symbol is the mental/emotional symbol. This symbol is used to deepen the connection between the giver and receiver to invite information to come forth that might be useful and appropriate for the receiver on their healing journey.

Catherine explains her experience of Level 1 and two attunements:

> *During the Reiki 1 initiation, I felt my energy channel open to about 5 cm and it resembled a white light as the energy came through. For a long time, I felt the energy circulate and it had the effect of straightening, reaching, and opening to the universal energy.*

During the Level 2 initiation, my channel definitely got bigger; I "saw" it grow to 10 cm in diameter. The intensity and power of the energy coming through my hands when I use the symbols is very strong.

Level 3

Alexandra, a Reiki level 3 student, shares:

Thank you so much for this opportunity to be a part of the most wonderful and illuminating spiritual experience I ever had in my life, the Reiki third level attunement I received in November 2009.

It was a breathtaking adventure of discovery to the land of the unknown. From the time we meditated as we began the day, I felt borne on wings of energy and I let them carry me through the rest of the journey. I experienced amazing things along the way: feeling stillness and becoming a part of it; sensing an immense power of energy field around me and dissolving into it; feeling tiny and yet big before the Universe; feeling united with everyone in the room; connected by the energy with the Universe and God; being in reverence before God, Masters and guides; feeling love for everyone around, for the whole of humanity; and feeling grateful for every precious second of this special day.

Thank you for an opportunity to learn new things and introducing us to the sacred Reiki 3 knowledge and for helping me to take one step further and higher on the endless path of spiritual growth. Thank you for creating this special event. I feel happy to have met such wonderful, special, kind, and interesting people whom I felt I knew all my life. I think every human being is the most wonderful miracle and when we are together and united, we can make a difference in the world.

I lost the sense of time and space that day and it passed by in one breath. In the end I even felt a little sad that the adventure was over. It was the most special day of my SOUL journey. From all my heart, with sincere respect and gratitude - Alexandra

At the third level, the student receives another powerful attunement and is taught some hand positions to help focus the energy and consciousness, as well as two more techniques to apply Reiki. He also learns the first master symbol which is a powerful symbol that invites expansion and light.

Once again, the principles are reviewed, questions are answered, and the students share experiences.

At this level, I begin to assign homework in the form of questions to reflect upon. I also request reports on two of several in-person and distance treatments. This ensures that the students actually practice to allow a deepening of all that has been learned to date and to take the time to study and report on the experience of giving and receiving treatments. I review and comment the assignments and return them to the students. I only issue the certificate at a final individual session with each student during which any questions are addressed and at which the student is invited to share their experience and journey of self-healing. Not all Reiki Masters provide this follow-up and guidance. I have found that at this level, this is invaluable for the student/practitioner who by now usually is interested in practicing Reiki more regularly or even professionally.

Level 4: Master/Teacher

Not everyone takes the Master/Teacher level with an intention to teach. Some take it for the personal growth that it offers before discovering, as I did, that they want to share it with others.

In order to be admitted into the Master/Teacher level, the Reiki Master must ensure that the candidate has the right attitude and motivation. If the Reiki Master does not know the applicant, it will be necessary to meet. Each Reiki Master will have a personalized way of reviewing and accepting students.

The teaching at the Master/Teacher level starts with a powerful attunement ritual and the introduction of a new symbol. Teaching and attuning students is taught later when the time is right.

Some Reiki Masters offer the training over a period of time supported by homework assignments and regular meetings. Others offer the training without this support but hopefully remain available to answer questions and give guidance when needed.

Personally, I require that students study with me over a period of eight months to one year, starting with the initiation ritual and continuing with attending my classes as observers; practicing the art; doing the assigned readings, assignments, and associated reports on six of the thirty treatments done over that time period.

The master students work at their own pace and benefit from ongoing contact with me, supported by review and comments on the work submitted. This ensures that the students integrate the teachings and can attend classes free of having to teach or learn the material. They are then available to take in what I say and how I teach without any pressure.

In addition, I coach them on starting their own practice and how to develop a clientele. They are required to attend and then perhaps lead a Reiki Share, which is a get-together of Reiki practitioners and sometimes newcomers to Reiki to share experiences, meditate, ask questions, and exchange treatments.

The training is complete when the students have met all the requirements; have integrated the heart and soul of the method; and will be able to receive, accompany, support, and guide potential students through the different levels from novice to Master/Teacher. I can then rest assured that they will faithfully transmit the learning to their own students with dedication, heart, and experience.

It does happen that I, or the students themselves, discover that they are not ready to take on this responsibility or are not suited to be a teacher and decide not to complete the training. They are supported in this process as needed.

All my students are encouraged to register with a recognized Reiki association.

Twenty-one days of integration

After completing each level, the student is encouraged to do a period of purification and integration lasting twenty-one consecutive days during which a Reiki treatment is done every day.

The sudden rise in the vibratory level from the attunements starts a continuous process of releasing toxins, held emotions, and negative energies which is supported by the self-treatment during these twenty-one days.

This integration process can be very smooth or it can be a period of vivid dreams, mood changes, strange sensations, or strong emotions, (anger, intense joy, etc.).

These are signs of integration and inner transformation. Paying attention to what is happening may reveal important messages that will support beneficial and necessary change. Keeping a journal during this period to record thoughts, emotions, and reactions will allow the student to reflect on and track progress.

Abundance through Reiki (Horan, 1995) contains exercise that can be very beneficial during this period.

Sabine, a Reiki level 2 student, shares:

My twenty-one-day period after level 2 was a little difficult in the last part, at about seven to ten days I was feeling sad and depressed, but this disappeared on day twenty-two, coinciding with my menstrual cycle. It was odd, but I've come to accept odd things can happen in these processes.

Summary of Chapter 3

Traditional Reiki was made popular by Mrs. Hawayo Takata, who learned it from Dr. Hayashi, a disciple of Usui. It can be learned in three or four levels depending on the lineage of the Master/Teacher.

The attunement, an energetic transmission given by the Reiki Master, creates an increase in the level of vibration of the energy field of the initiate that facilitates and augments the capacity to channel and transmit the energy. It is this attunement that acts as a catalyst for personal transformation.

Some extensions of traditional Reiki have been created by Masters who received additional information and symbols or have added techniques to the basic traditional method.

Reiki is transmitted by a simple laying-on of hands in person or at a distance. No other technique is needed or taught. Sacred symbols, learned from level 2 onwards, allow a connection at a distance, increase the power of the treatment, and create a deeper connection between the giver and the receiver.

At the Master/Teacher level, one is allowed to transmit the teachings to students of all levels.

CHAPTER 4

APPLYING REIKI: GUIDELINES FOR THE PRACTITIONER

As a Reiki practitioner, your prime objective is to be a clear channel for the client and to be as non-directive as possible. Although the Reiki practitioner is not practicing therapy, learning to create a safer and more loving healing container will increase the effectiveness of the treatment and will have a therapeutic effect.

As practitioner, this chapter will help you become aware of the many aspects that may come up between you and your clients while giving a treatment. It also addresses many questions that are brought up by students during the courses.

I will begin by addressing the relational aspects to consider. The healing space, ambiance, and equipment also have a significant impact on the treatment.

You do not need to have mastered all these before starting a professional practice. You will always be growing as a practitioner as you gain experience.

The practitioner/client relationship

The right use of power

The Right Use of Power (Barstow, 2007) is the title of a book written by about the dynamics of power in the client/practitioner relationship. As soon as you enter into a client/practitioner relationship, there is a strong probability that either or both of you will fall into unconscious roles. Often, the client gives the practitioner a lot of power. And some practitioners unknowingly look to "ego build" with their clients.

It is, therefore, important for the practitioner to be aware that a power dynamic exists so that the practitioner can watch for it, perhaps name it, and continually work to empower the client.

The Right Use of Power is based on experiential learning and is structured so that the reader can become aware of the potential traps in the client/practitioner relationship and the ways practitioners can empower clients while also claiming their own power as a practitioner.

Barstow explains that it can be just as damaging not to own your power as it is to give it away, either as a client or a practitioner.

Presence and non-doing

Wisdom without words,
born of inner silence,
carried within the heart,
dispensed with Loving Kindness.
This is true medicine. (Author Unknown)

This is one aspect that I continually stress in my teaching. In Reiki, the more you develop presence with yourself, the more you will be able to be with your client. The less you do and worry about during the treatment, the more effective it will become. Having set a clear intention to be there for the person's highest good, there is nothing more to do but trust that the divine intelligence of the client will absorb and direct the Reiki energy that you make available where it is required for healing, at the client's own pace.

This means not pushing, pulling, or otherwise manipulating the energy but rather letting your inner knowing and intuition guide you in the process.

You may find your mind wandering all over the place as you are trying to be present. If this happens, just bring yourself back gently and with compassion as soon as you notice it. The tendency is for new practitioners to close their eyes, assuming that perceiving will be easier with the eyes shut. Often this will invite the mind to stray. Instead, keep your eyes slightly open with a soft focus, and close them occasionally when needed. This will help you to stay more present.

In the healing profession, we often do not get feedback from our clients. Following up is kept to a minimum in order to respect the client's privacy and healing journey; therefore I seldom follow up with clients who do not return because I trust that they will know when to return if they need to. Not so long ago, I was reminded of the importance of simple presence. I got an email from a client I had seen only once several months earlier and whom I had not heard back from. She wanted to thank me for the one session that we had, saying that this one treatment had been a deciding factor in initiating major life changes. She stated "no one had ever been present with me in that way." Receiving this email helped me to trust and confirm that just being there is enough.

"Let the Doing come from the Being" is a quote I put up on my fridge as a constant reminder.

Healthy boundaries with clients

In order to be the best channel for healing, you need to get yourself completely out of the way. Your client's healing becomes the priority, and how you position yourself in the relationship will have an impact on the healing progress. There is always transference happening between you and the client (see the section on supervision in Chapter 5), and, most often, it is not conscious. If you develop a friendship with the client, there is a danger that you or the client will prioritize the relationship rather than the healing journey.

Setting and maintaining healthy boundaries is a skill you will need to develop as you begin to work with clients.

Shifting a practitioner/client relationship to a friendship sometimes happens and can be healthy if it is a mutually clear and conscious choice and if the transition is given the necessary time and support. Some schools of thought recommend as much as two years before allowing this change to take place. This way, all aspects can be considered, brought to consciousness, and discussed by both parties.

Healing is an "inside" job and the responsibility of the client

Healing is an "inside" job assisted by "outside" factors. When there is a physical injury of some kind (fracture, disease, burn) or some distress, help is administered in the way of drugs, splints, casts, surgery, psychotherapy, or some other form of "outside" assistance. But it is the body that heals, not what is administered; healing is from the inside. The same holds true for any emotional, psychic, mental, or spiritual healing. It happens at whatever level the person is ready for at that moment.

The practitioner does not control or direct the healing. He or she is simply available as an antenna or a channel for the energy, which then becomes available to the person receiving. This provides a template that the person can choose to follow or not. Being available for the client does not mean that you carry the responsibility. It is the client who is responsible for his or her healing journey, not the practitioner.

Healing may occur during the treatment or later—the same day or in a few days, months, or years. The Reiki treatment may simply set the stage for healing to occur.

A collaboration between client and practitioner

The client/practitioner relationship is a collaborative venture and the more you trust that the client has the necessary resources within, the more you will be able to "let go and let Reiki" do the work.

The need to fix, the habit of looking for what's wrong

Beware of the need to fix and look for what is wrong as the client walks into your office. As a helping professional, it is easy (and probably habitual) to categorize the client into all the little boxes and labels we may have learned in various trainings.

Instead, see if you can look for strengths and resources the moment the client walks into your office. What do you notice that lets you know you won't have to "work so hard" with this person? Can you trust that the client has everything inside and knows what is needed? Can you let go of results?

The Hakomi method (see Appendix G) teaches to look for what is nourishing as you interact with a client and that doing so will actually foster loving presence.

Know your limits

It could be that the client's condition is beyond what you are comfortable working with or he or she is a person with whom you are simply not comfortable.

You are perfectly free to take care of yourself and choose the clients with whom you work. Forcing yourself to work with persons with whom you are not comfortable will not benefit them. By referring them to a colleague, another health professional, or another approach, you will also be modeling self-responsibility, self-care, and healthy boundaries.

Preparing for clients and treating them

Before receiving your client, you will need to be centered and in a state of being that will be most conducive to give a treatment. The following are some of the things that you can do to prepare.

Come into contact with yourself

First, take some time to see how you are and what is present for you in the moment. Is there any unfinished business that is taking up a lot of space and that might prevent you from being totally present? Are there strong emotions left over from an interaction with another person? Is your physical condition preventing you from being fully present? If so, see if you can allow these things to be there by acknowledging them, while remaining present with your client.

You may choose to meditate for a while to help you center and align. Following the breath calms and centers. I often use the simple exercise of breathing in to a count of four, holding for a count of four, and then releasing to a count of eight. This has the effect of regulating the nervous system and moving the focus away from the mind.

Another way to center is to voice the mantra "OM" on a slow out-breath, which helps to align the upper chakras. Feeling the vibration of your own voice as it resonates throughout your body is soothing and beneficial.

Experiment and find a way that works for you.

State of being conducive to giving treatments

Energy will flow from the stronger field to the weaker field, just as it does between the two batteries when you boost a car that won't start. You need to be in better condition than the client so that it is actually the client who gets the treatment and not the other way around. If you are very tired or physically not well, it may be better to postpone the session. This does not mean that a person who is unwell (chronic illness or condition) cannot give Reiki, but one should check in and assess their level of energy before giving.

If you are experiencing strong emotions from an interaction you have had with someone and cannot set them aside, it may also be better to postpone the treatment.

Let go of results

It is not possible to know the full impact of a Reiki treatment. We are not in control of the client's healing process, nor can we determine the effects of the treatment or when they will be experienced. We cannot predict on which level (physical, emotional, mental, psychic, or spiritual) the healing will take place. While we may witness results during the treatment, such as relaxation, emotional and physical release, or insights, there may be other results of which we are not aware, which will happen in their own time and we may never hear about them.

Letting go of results is not as simple as it sounds. Most of us have been trained to do, direct, and analyze. Our self-worth is often measured by results. Letting go of results is a humbling experience and requires surrendering (giving over) to a Higher Knowing and trusting the process.

This has been one of the biggest challenges in my apprenticeship as a healing facilitator; I need to continuously invoke the Witness so I can catch myself in the process of doing, directing, or analyzing. The more I do this, the more I can get out of the way and trust, and the easier the work seems to become.

I often hear beginners ask their practice clients "Well, how did it go, what did you feel?" as soon as the Reiki treatment is over. It is better to allow some time for integration before the client gets up and allow any sharing to arise spontaneously. After some time, you may ask the more appropriate question "Is there anything you might like to share about your experience?"

Do not use your own energy to heal

If you notice that you are exhausted after giving a Reiki treatment, it may be due to some physical aspect, such as inappropriate table height, tiredness from standing for so long, leaning over because the client is not near enough to the side of the table that you are working on, holding your breath, or not relaxing as you are giving. It is quite OK to sit down as you are giving treatments, although it may be more difficult to feel well grounded in the sitting position.

It could also be that you are forcing the energy, using your own energy, and/or working very hard with your mind and trying too hard to perceive and understand what is going on during the treatment.

Beginners often overuse their third eye and furrow their brow in concentration, trying to see or perceive the energy and trying to do it "right." The shoulders and upper arms are often tensed up, which restricts the energy flow and brings on fatigue.

As you are giving a treatment, keep monitoring your posture and relaxing any tensions in your body. This will enhance the energy flow and transmission. And don't forget to breathe! Scan periodically to check your grounding and whether you are focusing intensely with any of your chakras. Reset your intention and even out your attention to all your chakras as you do this.

Set your clear intention

Intention is one of the most powerful tools I know. Take some time to set a clear and effortless intention to be present for your client's highest good.

These simple words are powerful "I set my clear intention to be fully present for my client, get myself out of the way, and surrender to the Divine and to his or her healing journey."

Grounding

Alexander Lowen and John Pierrakos coined the word "grounding" while developing Bioenergetics.

Grounding means being fully in your body and connected to the earth. It means feeling your feet on the ground and the earth's support. Being grounded allows you to tap into its very low and beneficial vibrations, thus making them available for you and for your client. Since grounding is such an important part of being alive, it is good to develop a strong sense of it.

Being grounded will greatly add to the Reiki energy coming through the crown chakra and channeled to the palms of the hands. Grounding is the first step in preparing your energy field to be more connected and a stronger channel for the Reiki and Earth energies.

In *A Path with Heart* (Kornfield, 1993) the author explains that it is very important to be well anchored in the root chakra, or grounded, whenever we meditate or otherwise work with the upper chakras.

Grounding can be progressively strengthened in three steps, which I like to refer to as Grounding 1-2-3. Here are the steps:

1. - First, relax your back and keep your head level. Softly focus on the floor with your eyes. With your feet parallel and about shoulder width apart, bend your knees slightly so that they are not locked to allow the energy to move up the legs. Move your whole body, particularly the pelvis and legs, thus bringing your consciousness down to the lower part of your body. Many of us tend to keep the energy up around the head.

Feel your feet on the ground and spread your toes so that you get maximum contact. Find your center front to back and feel your feet and your body completely supported by the earth. Then put all your weight on one foot and feel that connection. Do the same with the other foot and return to center. Take some deep breaths all the way down to your abdomen. Put your hands on your abdomen and feel them move with each breath. On the next breath, imagine that your legs are hollow and that the breath reaches all the way down to your toes.

2. - Next, imagine that there are roots growing in the form of two large cones from the underside of both your feet and that they penetrate the floor, the foundations of the building, the different layers of the earth—earth, sand, rocks, crystals—all the way down to the center of the earth. Imagine or see the roots encircling the center of the earth and filling the whole cone, front, back, sides, and center. Then intend and see these roots connecting with the consciousness of the earth and absorbing that energy of nourishment and support. Let that energy move up the roots like the sap moves up the roots of a tree. Let it fill your

whole auric field and body. You may feel heat and see colors as you do this, or not. Keep breathing deeply.

3. - The last and very important step is to connect with your center of intention, a point in the center of your body just below the naval, about the size of a golf ball and in the shape of a walnut. Barbara Brennan (1993) introduces and describes this in *Light Emerging*. She says that this point is where you hold your intention for being incarnated in this life and in this body. Connect to it by bringing your fingers of both hands together on this point and letting them penetrate your body energetically until they connect to it. Once connected, intend to create a connection between this point and the energetic consciousness of the earth at its center. Align your intention from this connection to be fully present for your client.

Keep this grounding stance and intention as you move from one position to the next during the treatment. You will notice that your connection and the flow of energy will be much more powerful. Many of my students get very hot when they first practice this way of grounding.

Open your energy field

Next, prepare your field to run more energy by opening the chakras so that each one can be fully available to allow in the energy and the unique vibration associated with that chakra. You can do this simply by bringing your consciousness to each one and breathing into them so that they naturally open, starting with the root chakra at the perineum. If you are familiar with the colors associated with each one, you can bring them in also as you connect.

1st chakra – red

2nd chakra – orange

3rd chakra – lemon yellow

4th chakra – spring green

5th chakra – sky blue

6th chakra – indigo

7th chakra – violet or white

Since the chakras are also receptors of information, you are increasing your capacity to receive information that may be available as you give the treatment.

Meet your client

New clients may not be familiar with Reiki and may be nervous and perhaps skeptical about this "weird" new age treatment. They may have been recommended by one of your clients, or colleagues, or perhaps a spouse. They may not even be sure they want to be there. They may have come because they are curious or because they have a condition they are struggling with and have tried everything else.

Allow a little extra time in your schedule for new clients. Pay attention and be in unconditional presence. Meet them wherever they are in their process. If they are new to Reiki, you will want to explain to them what it is and what they might expect during the treatment.

It will be important to let them know that Reiki is a complementary and sometimes alternative treatment approach, but that they should consult a health professional for any questions about their condition, as you cannot diagnose with Reiki or prescribe any medication. You can let them know that Reiki will not interfere with any other treatments they are undergoing but will rather work to support them and perhaps accelerate the healing process. Let them know that they do not have to believe or "buy into" Reiki. All they need is to have an intention to heal and be open to this new experience.

Developing good listening skills and practicing loving presence will help them feel more at ease with you and the treatment.

Once you have informed them about Reiki, inquired about their reason for being there, and answered their questions, you can tell them how the treatment will take place. Let them know that emotions can come up during the treatment as they are released from the blocks holding them in. Reassure them that this is a sign of healing taking place and that you will be present with them throughout while continuing to transmit Reiki. Often when clients experience strong emotions they tend to hold their breath. Breathing into emotions will help them move through and release the emotions much more easily.

Then you can invite them on to the table and make sure they are comfortable before starting.

Set intention with the client

Once you have made sure that your client is comfortable, invite him or her to set intention for the session in whatever way feels appropriate. Most often, I will use one or all these invitations:

- I invite you to open to receiving this energy of divine consciousness and unconditional love so that it might clear, balance, charge, and repair any areas that need it.

- You may invite any spiritual friends, guides, angels, and the presence of ascended masters to be present. If it is appropriate for you, you can also invite them to assist during the treatment.

- You may invite the Universe to put on your path all the experiences, information, messages, persons, events, books, or anything else that you are ready to experience that might contribute to your healing journey so that you may return to wholeness and continue to share the essence and gift of who you are with the world around you. Let this be effortless and fun. I often notice the client sigh and smile at the "effortless and fun" part of this invitation.

Then, after making sure you are grounded and that you have set clear intention for being present, you can breathe into your chakras and start the treatment.

To touch or not to touch

First, check with your client to see if it is okay for you to lay your hands directly on the treatment positions. This is important because some clients may not be comfortable with being touched in some or all parts of the body, especially if they have suffered abuse.

Although Reiki energy will flow into the client's field with the hands on or off the body, I strongly recommend, if the client allows it, to actually be in contact with the client at all times, with a solid enough pressure so that you can feel the client and the client can feel you. Touch can be a very significant aspect of accompanying someone. Touch lets them know you are really there with them and for them. It enhances the heart connection between the two of you. We are not touched enough in a caring way in our society.

You may find that you feel the flow of energy less with your hands directly on the client. If this is the case, remember that the client is the priority and anything that will enhance the connection will also enhance the treatment. If you have resistance to touch, be curious about why this is so. It may be worth looking at this with your therapist or supervisor.

If you have permission to touch, lay your hands on the positions such that you feel a solid contact between your hands and the client's body. Tell the client to let you know if the pressure becomes uncomfortable and check in from time to time.

When you change positions, do so one hand at a time so that you are always in contact with the client.

Sink your hands energetically

Once you have your hands on the client on any given position, allow your hands to sink energetically into the client's field. Imagine that they penetrate deeply into the body. This will deepen your connection and the client's experience, and the energy will flow even more. Breathe deeply as you are doing this, and ground.

Perceiving and feeling

When you give a Reiki treatment, you may or may not feel the energy and may or may not receive or perceive information from the client as you work. This is of secondary importance to being present and giving Reiki.

Many of us have a strong need to know, feel, see, or otherwise perceive. If we don't, we begin to discount our ability and doubt ourselves, the effectiveness of the treatment and our self-worth. When we look too hard and search too much, we do not appreciate or even notice what we do perceive because it does not look like what we think it should. This is a vicious circle because the more we strive to perceive, the less we can be aware of what we actually do perceive because our attention is elsewhere.

There are actually about twelve different ways to perceive the energy field depending on which of our chakras are attuned and open to receiving. It can be felt kinesthetically, emotionally, or intuitively. It can be felt as a feeling of love; experienced as a sense of taste or smell; heard as a sound or a form of guidance; or seen in forms and colors in the same way we see everything around us. You may see on your mind screen—pictures or images, symbols or shapes that come into your mind as you work. Or, it can be direct knowing.

For a very long time, I did not feel the energy flow and wanted so much to see the energy field. Even though I did not feel much, I could see that clients benefited from the treatments and that was enough to keep me going. The more I am able to surrender to not knowing, the more I seem to feel and perceive. I have often found that it is when I am not searching that I get surprised. Fortunately, I did not wait to see and feel before starting to give treatments.

As I continue to give treatments, I am aware that my strongest senses are intuition, the ability to feel emotions, and a sense of direct knowing. Sometimes I get a picture in my mind of what I need to see while working on a particular area (muscle, organ, bone, etc.). Lately, I have been starting to see different colors around my clients or see their hands change color as they talk but this is not yet clear enough to make any interpretations.

We all have our different strengths in the way we perceive the energy. This will likely improve the more you work with the energy.

Hot and cold spots

A question I often get is "What does it mean when the place where I have my hands is hot or cold?" It could mean one of several things.

If the area feels hot, generally it is an indication that Reiki energy is being absorbed. The hotter your hands are, the more energy is being drawn into the client's energy field.

If the position feels cold, there may be a block in this area; the energy is not being absorbed or is being pushed away. This can happen when the chakra is "closed" or in protection mode and is pushing and/or resisting. The muscles in an area of the body that is tensed up will constrict the blood vessels and impair the circulation. This area will then feel cold to touch.

A cold spot can also indicate an energy leak. Joints, such as the ankles, knees, and shoulders, are typical places where energy leaks out of the field.

Types of information received: to share or not to share

If you do receive/perceive information as you are giving a treatment, it can come in different forms. Some of the information can be factual and some can be symbolic.

Whether you are feeling something or receiving information, the first thing to do is to ask the question "is this about me or for me, or is it about or for the client, or both?" For example, if you are on the third chakra (solar plexus) you might get a feeling of nausea. It could be that the client is not feeling nauseous at the time but that the nausea is connected with some past issue. It could be that being in contact with this chakra brings up something for you in your process. Or it could be an issue common to both of you. Asking the question may allow you to become clear. If it is clear that it is not about you, then simply note it for the time being and do not interpret it, as you can never be sure of its significance for the client.

The question then arises, "Do I share this information or not?" The key to answering this question is whether the information will be useful for the client and whether this is the right time. Also check whether you are sharing for the client's benefit or whether it is your ego that wants to show off and impress the client—engage your witness.

If you are not sure, then err on the safe side and do not share it, at least for the moment. If you do feel it is appropriate to share, then you might say something like "When I was at this position, I felt this, or this came into my mind. I don't know what it is but perhaps it has some meaning for you." Clients will often ask what I sensed during the treatment when they get up from the table. Often I have nothing to tell them and just say so.

Treatment and positions

The various positions for giving a Reiki treatment are illustrated in Appendix A. The basic protocol is generally the same but may vary from teacher to teacher and from book to book. The standard positions on the major chakras and joints are those areas of the body where the energy penetrates most easily into the energy field.

It is suggested to treat for three to a maximum of five minutes per position. As you become proficient at giving treatments, you will begin to follow your intuition. The positions and the amount of time you spend on each will vary from one treatment to the next and from one client to another.

When giving Reiki, keep your fingers together and the palm flat. I like to use the image of a dead spider lying completely flat on the body, with all the points of the hand touching the body. Remember to keep a solid contact with the client so that they can feel your presence. When changing from one position to the next, change one hand at a time to maintain that contact. This lets the client know you are present, which will be significant for those who may have experienced and suffered from abandonment.

Treating the self

The positions I teach for the self are listed below. The associated chakra is listed next to the position where applicable.

If you do all these positions with the suggested time of three minutes per position, the treatment will take fifty minutes or so. It is always best to do all the positions first and then treat other areas of the body to which you may be drawn. This clears and prepares the field for deeper work. If you don't have the time available, you can just give yourself a shorter treatment.

Note to novices: If you have not yet been initiated, try these positions on yourself anyways while setting a healing intention. You will most likely feel some heat in your hands, relax and have a sense of wellbeing.

After grounding, breathing into your chakras and setting your intention, activate any symbols you have learned before you start the treatment.

Front of the body – 13 positions

- Head (crown), 7th chakra
- Covering the eyes (third eye), 6th chakra
- Temples, 6th chakra
- Back of the head, 6th chakra

- Back of the neck, upper shoulders, 5th chakra
- Throat, 5th chakra
- Heart, 4th chakra
- Solar plexus, 3rd chakra
- Lower belly (just above the pubic bone), 2nd chakra
- Root, hand on groin, 1st chakra
- Knees
- Ankles (on the joint)
- Soles of the feet

<u>Back of the body – 3 positions</u>

Reactivate the symbols before you start on the back if you have level 2 or higher.

- Back of the solar plexus, 3rd chakra
- Lower back (lumbar area), 2nd chakra
- Root (hand on sacrum and coccyx), 1st chakra

Then add any position that needs it—organ, injury, surgery, muscle tension, pain, etc.

<u>Sweep</u>

After completing all the positions, you can do a final clearing by sweeping your aura with your hands from head to toe two or three times in order to send any remaining stagnant energy to Mother Earth or the Universe.

Closing the treatment

Once you have finished, honor yourself for the work you have done and the time you have given yourself and give thanks to the Source for its energy.

Treating another person

The positions I teach to treat another person are listed below. The associated chakra is listed next to the position where applicable. These differ slightly from treating the self. The crown chakra is omitted but can be added if you wish.

It is suggested to wash your hands before and after the treatment to clear the energy and for proper hygiene.

If you do all the positions with the suggested time of three minutes per position, the treatment will take about forty-five minutes. You can give a shorter treatment depending on the available time.

After grounding, breathing into your chakras, and inviting the client to set intention, activate any symbols you have learned in level 2 or higher over the crown chakra before you start the treatment.

Ask the client to be as close as possible to the side of the table you will be working from so that your back is straight and comfortable during the treatment. This will be the side on which your dominant hand is towards the lower part of the client's body (if you are right handed, you will place yourself on the client's right side).

For the first few positions, you will be standing at the head of the client. When working from the side, keep your dominant hand in front of your non-dominant hand. This will make it easier to transition to the groin position at the root chakra. (See the pictures in Appendix A).

Remember to let your hands "sink" into the energy field and to periodically scan your presence and grounding.

Front of the body – 11 positions

- Covering the eyes (third eye), 6th chakra, (use light pressure at this position)
- Temples, 6th chakra
- Back of the head, 6th chakra
- Throat, 5th chakra, (use light pressure at this position)
- Heart, 4th chakra
- Solar plexus, 3rd chakra
- Lower belly (just above the pubic bone), 2nd chakra
- Root, hand on groin, 1st chakra
- Knees
- Ankles (on the joint)
- Soles of the feet (on the solar plexus point, just below the ball of the foot)

Back of the body – 4 positions

- Back of the heart, 4th chakra
- Back of the solar plexus, 3rd chakra
- Lower back (lumbar area), 2nd chakra
- Root (hand on sacrum and coccyx), 1st chakra

Then give additional Reiki to any position to which you feel drawn or that was specifically requested by the client (organ, injury, surgery, muscle tension, pain, etc.).

Sweep

Once you have completed all the positions, you can do a final clearing by sweeping the aura with your hands from head to toe two or three times in order to send any remaining stagnant energy to Mother Earth or the Universe. Do a sweep on each side of the body and one in the center.

Closing the treatment

Once you have finished, place one hand at the crown chakra and another at the root chakra and separate your hands while backing away two or three feet from the client. Disconnect energetically by standing with your hands facing the client and hold the intention of giving the healing responsibility back to the client. Honor yourself for the work you have done and give thanks.

Let the client integrate for a few minutes before inviting her or him to get up. It is a good idea to offer water at this point.

Mental/emotional treatment (two positions)

This two-position treatment can be remarkably effective. It can be used when time is not available for a full treatment or just as an alternate way of treating. The first position is with the dominant hand on the forehead and the other on the back of the head. The second position is with both hands cupping the head. Each position is held for about ten minutes.

As with the standard treatment, prepare your energy field by grounding and breathing into your chakras and then activate any symbols you may have learned before starting.

End the treatment by doing the sweep and disconnect in the same way described above for a standard treatment.

What I like about this treatment is its simplicity: only two positions to remember and to track. This frees you to just be present. You will be amazed at how the energy flows where it needs to go. My level 2 students are often amazed at the depth of relaxation and intensity of this way of treating. It is a great confirmation that Reiki can be effective in any position.

Quick treatment

Another simple and fun way to treat is by giving what I call the "quick treatment." This consists of laying the hands first on the shoulders and then on the seven major chakras for just a short time (a few seconds to one minute each). This treatment is most easily done when the client is sitting on the edge of a chair so that you have access to the front and back of the body. This treatment works great at the office or at home when someone is stressed out or has a headache.

Again, take the time to ground and breathe into your chakras.

These are the positions:

First, stand behind the client and do the first two positions.

- Shoulders (both hands)
- Crown, 7th chakra (both hands)

Then move to one side using one hand on the front and the other on the back of the body and do:

- Third eye, 6th chakra (one hand on the forehead and the other on the nape)
- Throat, 5th chakra
- Heart, 4th chakra

- Solar plexus, 3rd chakra

- Lower belly (just above the pubic bone), 2nd chakra

- Root, 1st chakra (one hand between the knees beaming energy into the root chakra and the other on the sacrum)

End the treatment by simply backing away and disconnecting energetically from the client, honoring, and giving thanks.

Treatment on any position

Reiki can be effective when done on a single position, for example, while simply holding someone's hand and letting the Reiki energy flow if they are in bed (e.g., at the hospital) or while treating an injury.

Distance treatments

As quantum physics confirms, everything is energy and we are all interconnected. We can connect to anyone anywhere by simply using our intention. In level 2, a symbol is taught that is used to connect at a distance.

When sending Reiki from a distance, all you need is to know to whom or what you intend to send Reiki (person, object, world situation, animal, or Mother Earth). You can use a picture to help you feel more connected, but this is not necessary.

A traditional distance treatment takes ten to fifteen minutes but can be longer.

Distance Reiki to individuals

Permission

You must have the permission of the person or object before sending Reiki to respect free will and not impose healing on anyone.

It is preferable to have verbal permission and set it up so that the receiver is available and in a quiet state of mind when receiving. This will enhance the possibility for the person to be aware of any insights, feelings, or other sensations. When this is not possible, for example, in the case where the person cannot be available, has not been contacted, is in a coma, or has died, then a treatment can still be sent if non-verbal permission has been obtained as described below.

Even if you have the verbal permission, it is recommended to also ask for non-verbal permission (of the soul, or what could be called telepathically).

How to ask for permission

Close your eyes and say internally: "I ask (name of the person) the permission to send a Reiki treatment by distance," or "Is it appropriate for me, and do I have permission at this time, to send a distance Reiki treatment to (name of person)." Keep your eyes closed and wait for the answer to come to you. It may come in the form of a clear yes or no or in the form of a symbol, such as a door opening, a light, a good feeling that you interpret as a yes or a door closing, darkness, or an uncomfortable feeling that you interpret as a no. Trust your feeling and act accordingly.

If you get no signal, you can ask that the treatment be received of free will and send it anyways, with the intention that the Reiki energy be directed elsewhere if it is not welcome. Remember that the important thing is to respect the client's free will and not fall victim to your ego that may want to "force" healing or change on someone.

If the answer is "yes"

Use your thighs or any object such as a stuffed animal to represent the person. The thigh or object is used to focus your attention and keep you present. If you use the thigh, the right thigh can represent the front of the body and the left thigh can represent the back. Alternately, you can visualize the person miniaturized in the palm of your hand.

Prepare yourself in the same way as you would for an in-person treatment and then activate any symbols you have learned. Lay your hands on the "front" of the body for approximately seven minutes and then on the "back" of the body for approximately seven minutes. Reactivate the symbols before doing the "back" of the body.

Alternately, you can perform Reiki on each of the body positions as if the person were lying there in front of you. This will take longer, of course, because you will be doing all the positions, but it may allow a deeper connection to the client and you may get more specific information as you give the treatment.

Experiment with either way and see which one you find more comfortable.

End of treatment

Once you have completed all the positions, place your hands facing each other 12 to 18 inches apart. Bring your hands toward each other until they touch, at which point you disconnect energetically. If you feel resistance, pause and communicate with the person telepathically. The person may feel insecure so just reassure and continue closing.

When finished, honor yourself and give thanks.

Don't forget the exchange.

<u>Distance Reiki to situations, world events, etc.</u>

When sending Reiki to situations, world events, etc., you do not need the permission of each individual because you are sending Reiki to the collective. You can simply request permission to send to the collective. Reiki will act on the collective for everyone's highest good. Generally this means that the situation will evolve more harmoniously and with less conflict.

Otherwise, the treatment is done in the same way as described above for an individual.

Treating children

Children are more receptive to energy and absorb it readily; they have less resistance and are more spontaneous and intuitive. The treatment for a child can be shorter but just as effective.

As Reiki is energy of unconditional love given through touch, it greatly reinforces the bond between the child and the parent. It adds effectiveness to a parent's instinctive reaction to apply a hand on an injury or sore. The soothing and calming effect of Reiki helps a child get to sleep more quickly.

The child will probably let you know when he or she has received enough energy on one or all positions. The hands can cover several positions at once depending on the size of the child.

An unborn child can be treated in the womb by putting the hands on the belly.

Group treatments

Group treatment is a wonderful way to share Reiki with other practitioners or to give an "intense" treatment to one person. The treatments at Dr. Hayashi's clinic were often given by a group of practitioners.

A group treatment involves several practitioners giving a treatment while a "session leader" coordinates the changing of positions. Group treatments are often done in Reiki Shares, where each participant takes a turn at being treated by the others. It is a wonderful experience to have so many hot hands on the body.

To begin a group treatment, the participants do a short centering exercise, such as the meditation, "OM," or breathing as described in an earlier section, and align their intention to act as a harmonious group for the highest good of the client. One person lies on the table to receive and the other participants take their places around the table. The person at the head coordinates the beginning of the treatment and the changes of the positions while keeping track of the time.

For example, if three persons treat one person on the table, they would take the following places:

- One person at the head to treat the eyes, the temples, the back of the head, and the throat.

- A second person on the side to treat the thorax—the heart, solar plexus, sacral chakra, and root.

- A third person at the lower body to treat the knees, ankles, and feet.

Depending on the client's needs, the positions of the back can also be done.

The principle of exchange is automatically respected as everyone gives and receives.

Treating animals

Animals love and respond extremely well to Reiki. Since they have a chakra system similar to humans, similar positions can be used, that is, the major energy centers and joints. Just like children, animals will also let you know when they have had enough and simply leave.

The hands can cover several positions at once depending on the size of the animal. For small animals, simply hold them in the palm of your hands. Animals in a cage can be treated by simply holding the hands on either side of the cage or aquarium and beaming Reiki to them.

I once offered to give a Reiki treatment to a neighbor's dog suffering from a herniated disc. He was in so much pain that he would not let me approach him to lay my hands on his back; therefore, I did it from a sitting position a few feet away from him. The effect was noticeable; he progressively calmed down and lay on the floor and the treatment had a lasting impact.

This website: has beautiful illustrations of animal chakras (Also see Appendix A).
<www.patinkas.co.uk/Chakra_System_of_Animals/ch akra_system_of_animals.html>

Treating plants, gardens, spaces

Treat plants by cupping the hands around them if they are small, or just beam Reiki by turning your palms towards the plant. Treat a garden or a space by beaming to it with your palms facing the garden or space.

Frequency of treatments

How often should a person get a treatment? This depends on a number of factors, such as the severity of the condition, the availability of the practitioner and client, resources, etc.

Ideally, the treatments are given close together in the beginning and then at regular intervals after that, as this tends to result in a more pronounced effect. Some books suggest beginning with one treatment each day for four consecutive days to fully engage the healing process and give it momentum.

If I am working with someone with a serious condition such as cancer, I recommend that they come at least twice per week, depending on how advanced the cancer is.

As a general guideline, I suggest that clients come for four to six treatments. This will give them time to feel the effects and stabilize the energy field.

After an initial concentrated series of treatments, it is generally beneficial to receive treatments at regular intervals to provide ongoing support and reduce the likelihood of any recurrence. The treatments can be spaced out according to the client's needs, keeping in mind the intent to best serve the client and not foster dependency.

Effects of the treatment

Clients will usually get up from the table feeling relaxed as though waking from a deep sleep. Time will have all but disappeared.

Since there is quite a contrast between the state of the energy field before and after the first treatment it is very common that a client will feel the need to rest for a day or two afterwards as the body releases held toxins. As blocks and stagnant energy are released, numbed and tensed areas may become more sensitive for a time. This is referred to as a healing crisis; it results from the body adjusting and will usually subside in a couple of days. Meanwhile, resting and drinking a lot of water will assist in flushing out the toxins.

As the energy field becomes balanced and the chakras begin to open, the client's life experience is positively affected. This is because the chakras are the doorways through which we relate to our environment. Old images and beliefs will be challenged as the client reacts and responds in new, more nourishing ways. Sometimes, the pendulum swings way over before coming back to center. One of my clients was startled to see herself sharply reprimanding someone who was irritating her. Her habit had been to not take up space or express her needs. This only happened once or twice as she adjusted to her new way of being.

Tracking the progress of healing

After completing my training with Barbara Brennan, I created the Chakra Charting Method© to track the progress of healing by tabulating chakra readings and displaying them graphically. This innovative and state of the art system will be the subject of another book, but a glimpse of the method can be found in an article on my website:

<rolandberard.com/Production/EN/chartingHealing.htm>

The software can be purchased from the website. The method gives simple visual feedback and confirms how the energy field changes and becomes more harmonious with successive treatments. This tool can be used as a bridge between the Reiki practitioner and other health professionals.

Protecting and clearing your aura

A common concern for newcomers to Reiki is whether they will take on or be otherwise affected by whatever ails the client, such as negative energies, disease, or trauma.

This is not likely to happen, unless you have a personal dynamic of taking things on for others or have trouble saying no and setting limits.

You are not responsible for your client's healing and it is no reflection on you if "no results" are obtained. Your only responsibility is to be present with a clear intention to be a channel for the other's highest good. The rest belongs to the client. You might add this "clause" when setting your intention during your preparation.

Remember that energy flows from the stronger field to the weaker field. Being initiated into Reiki acts as a protection in itself as it raises the vibration of your energy field. In addition, if you have prepared your energy field by grounding and breathing into your chakras, chances are that your energy field is in a higher state of vibration and more harmonious than the person who has come to you for treatment. These, and the fact that both of your intentions are for the energy to flow from practitioner to client, will act to "protect" you from any negative transmissions.

Some practitioners are able to feel whatever the client is experiencing in their bodies or their emotions. This is a useful tool to perceive, but once the information has been received, it is okay to let it go without fearing that the client will "get it back." Trust that the treatment will take care of it, or not, depending on the client's healing path.

If you find yourself feeling that you have taken on something once the client has left, here are a few things you can do:

- Check and see if what you are feeling is exactly what the client came in with and set intention to let it go into the Earth or the Universe;

- Do a sweep of your aura;

- Use white sage or incense to purify your field;

- Change your clothes or take a shower;

- Imagine a violet Reiki rain pouring down on your field and washing any undesirable energy into the earth;

- Breathe it away;

- Take a bath with salt and baking soda. The salt will electrolyze the water and take away any charge and the baking soda will alkalize the water and also help to clear. Barbara Brennan (1993, p. 120) suggests using up to one pound (450 grams) of each and cautions to use warm (not hot) water. Now you know why you feel so good after swimming in the ocean.

If the situation persists, then I recommend that you see a therapist to help you look at your personal dynamics. I have often worked with students who have realized how their difficulty in setting healthy boundaries resulted in them taking on other peoples' problems. It has been very freeing for them to transform this dynamic and learn to let others be responsible for their own lives.

Healing space and accessories

Healing space

If you have the luxury of having a room in which to give treatments, you can set it up as a sacred healing space. Both you and your clients will benefit from the resulting ambiance. Enhance this space with sacred objects, inspiring colors, and pictures. The walls of my office are the colors of the chakras; clients immediately feel their effect when entering the space. If your office is used exclusively for treatments, the healing energy will remain clear and build over time.

However, Reiki can be done anywhere, lying or sitting, depending on the circumstances. Don't let the fact that you do not have a space prevent you from doing treatments; just make sure you are yourself comfortable while you are giving the treatment.

As a practitioner, you may find it more comfortable to have an office space. It is easier to set healthy boundaries with clients in the professional setting of an office. I used to see clients at home, but I have discontinued this practice after I realized that it tended to weaken the boundaries between my clients and me.

Periodically, you may need to clear the space. This can be done with white sage, beeswax, or incense, or by burning Epsom salts sprinkled with a capful of 100 proof alcohol. When clearing a space, spend some time in the corners and under the furniture as stagnant energy tends to accumulate in these places.

Equipment

Table

A kitchen counter, tabletop, folding table, or a bed can be used as a treatment table; however, they may not be very comfortable and their height cannot be adjusted. If you are using a collapsible banquet table, make sure the legs are secure; some have locking mechanisms that automatically fall into place when the table is set up.

Nowadays, good quality, light, collapsible, and portable massages tables are readily available and relatively inexpensive. Be sure to check the weight if you plan to move around a lot.

Choose a table that is wide enough so that the client's arms do not fall off the sides of the table. I like to use a table width of 70 cm (28 inches). Make sure the table is solid—those with wire supports have a good capacity for all types of clients. Have a close look at the clamps for the height adjustment to make sure that they cannot easily loosen and inadvertently collapse as your client climbs up on the table. I like the ones with two clamping screws or with a recessed area on the mating surfaces; this prevents the legs from collapsing if the screws ever become loose. Get into the habit of checking the table before the client gets on it.

A face rest and forearm support will add to the client's comfort.

Cushions, leg supports, blankets

Small things can make a big difference for your clients. Here are a few suggestions.

Client comfort can be enhanced with a bolster under the knees while lying on the back to reduce lower back stress and one under the ankles to reduce ankle stress while lying on the stomach. Small pillows of varying thicknesses will reduce neck stress.

The body temperature usually drops when a person lies down for some time and so the client may need to be covered when receiving a treatment. I have blankets in all the chakra colors; the clients are delighted to be able to select a color according to their moods. Surprisingly (or not!), they often choose a color related to the charka that needs attention that day.

Because the clients remain clothed during the treatments, it is not necessary to change the table cover from one client to the next, but some practitioners prefer to do this anyways as a way of clearing the energy between clients. Some practitioners use disposable or washable covers for the pillows.

Once the client is comfortably installed on the table, I suggest stretching the pant legs to remove the cloth folds from under the knees for added comfort.

Setting a favorable ambiance

Anything you can do to help the client relax will enhance the treatment. Soft lighting (stay away from fluorescent lights), colors, candles, incense, and music can all contribute to an atmosphere that will help the client be more available to whatever comes up during the treatment. Tibetan bells (tingshas) or Tibetan bowls can also clear space and set up good vibrations.

Incense will clear the space of negative energy and permeate it with an inspiring and pleasant fragrance. If you use incense, make sure it is of good quality and not perfumed artificially such as incense that has been made in ashrams in India or Nepal. My favorite is Nag Champa, which is readily available in bookstores, health food stores, and some pharmacies. Be aware that some people may be sensitive or allergic to incense.

Use incense sparingly, perhaps for a few minutes before the client arrives. When I started my practice, I would burn incense during the whole treatment; the room would fill with smoke and the smell was overpowering. I quickly learned that just a little incense is all that was needed.

Music will help most clients to relax, but it is a good idea to ask because silence is sometimes preferred. Use soft music without words or in a different language to minimize distractions. Mozart's music has often been cited as very beneficial for healing. My music selections are listed on my website to make them available to clients and students.

Appendix D lists some of the music I use during my sessions.

Summary of Chapter 4

Several factors need to be taken into consideration by the practitioner when giving a Reiki treatment. When a practitioner receives a client, he or she automatically falls into the role of therapist, with all the responsibilities that this entails. It is worthwhile for all practitioners to be aware of what might come up, whether or not they are practicing professionally.

The relationship between the practitioner and the client is one of the most important factors affecting the outcome of a Reiki treatment, much more so than in any specific technique. The presence of the practitioner both with himself or herself and with the client is crucial to the relationship.

A lot of power is given to the practitioner when a client comes for treatment. Being conscious of this, the practitioner can accompany the client on the healing journey by continually empowering the client through progressive sessions, knowing that healing comes from the inside and that the client has everything needed to heal. The work then becomes one of collaboration and the client remains involved in the healing journey, rather than being "fixed" by the practitioner.

The preparation of the practitioner before the treatment helps to set the ground for the session. Starting by connecting to him or herself to see what is present, putting aside anything that may get in the way of being fully present, the practitioner then aligns intention to be a clear channel and to be completely present for the highest good of the client.

The practitioner must let go of results and remember that he or she does not control the healing process but rather offers a healing energy template that can be integrated by the client in his or her own time. The practitioner must simply allow the energy to do its work and trust the client's process.

The practitioner's preparation, ambiance, touch, equipment, and accessories can all enhance the treatment.

After a treatment, the practitioner returns the responsibility for healing to the client and hangs on to none of what has transpired or what has been perceived. If ever the practitioner feels the need, there are several ways to clear his energy field after a treatment.

CHAPTER 5

INTEGRATING REIKI INTO YOUR LIFE AND WORKPLACE

This chapter explores the different ways of integrating Reiki into your life and workplace.

Reiki in your life

Daily practice

After giving yourself Reiki for the 21-day period of integration, you may take a liking to a daily treatment and may begin to use Reiki more and more in your life. Giving yourself Reiki as often as you can will keep your energy field balanced and impact your life.

You might also consider a daily practice of sending Reiki to one or more world situations, family members, and friends.

Ongoing activities

If you use Reiki often, it will become second nature, and you may start to send some ahead to activities in which you are involved.

When I was working as an engineering project manager, I would send distance Reiki to meetings that I was scheduled to participate in or lead. Whenever I attend or teach a course, or go for treatments or therapy, I send Reiki ahead to support the Higher Selves of everyone involved. I also send Reiki ahead of time to meetings with friends or colleagues when I am a bit nervous about how it might go.

Not a day goes by that I am not sending Reiki to someone or something. As I write this book, I regularly apply Reiki so that I can be inspired and write effortlessly.

With friends and colleagues

Reiki shares and exchanges are a wonderful way to stay in touch with friends and colleagues. A Reiki Share can be organized by any group of practitioners who want to practice and stay motivated. Often it is organized by a Reiki Master who might invite the sharing of experiences, lead a meditation, answer questions, and give guidance as required.

You can exchange with other practitioners using Facebook or other Internet sites—you can even start your own blog.

Joining an association is another way to stay in touch and be supported in your practice.

Reiki in your work

The workplace

Even if you do not have a Reiki practice, there are many ways that you can integrate Reiki into your workplace. You can give Reiki to your current files and projects, to meetings you have to attend, and to your teams and workgroups. You can clear your office space of stagnant energy using Reiki.

The business world is usually perceived as conservative and close-minded when it comes to talking about anything spiritual or emotional. Yet I found myself sharing my experiences and interest in Reiki with some of my engineering colleagues. To my surprise, many were more open-minded and curious than I would have ever imagined. Several of my current Reiki clients are practicing engineers.

112

Your current practice

Reiki can be integrated into your current practice, whether you are a holistic practitioner, a dentist, a hair stylist, or do some other kind of work. As a massage therapist or other hands-on health professional, integrating Reiki into your work will help clients to relax more and help to dissolve muscle tensions as you work.

Using Reiki can soothe anxious or fearful clients. Let your clients know that you have learned a new technique and would like to use it to help them relax and facilitate your work.

You will probably notice that your hands feel hotter whenever you put them on your clients and that your state of being will have changed as a result of the initiations and any treatments you have received, even when you are not specifically intending to use or transmit Reiki. Your clients will feel the difference.

Setting up a Reiki practice

You may eventually decide to start your own professional Reiki practice. This section gives some guidelines to help you set it up.

The Reiki courses do not address ethics and client relations; therefore, I recommend that you take a course to help you deal with common issues that come up as a helping professional. I also suggest that you join a Reiki association.

Starting a practice might seem daunting. Trust yourself—we are always learning, growing, and integrating new knowledge and skills as we gain experience. There will be times when the issue the client brings to the session will be one you have just worked through and with which you will be able to help.

I often joke that we call it a practice because we are always practicing and the clients are called patients because they patiently wait for us to get competent.

Setting up a business

A professional practice is a business and must meet government requirements for reporting income and collecting taxes where applicable. The advantage of running it as a business is that you can deduct the business expenses on your tax return. These include office supplies, office space (rental, part of your home, or both), office equipment (such as computers, telephone, and Internet), software, advertising and business development, travel, and any courses and conferences that you attend that qualify as professional development or are related to your profession.

You will have to keep track of all the expenses and keep supporting documentation on file. You will have to retain this documentation for the number of years required by the applicable laws. Setting up separate accounts and credit cards to keep track of your business income and expenses will greatly facilitate your bookkeeping.

Insurance

If you practice professionally, you may want to consider getting insurance for professional liability for errors and omissions and for civil liability in case anyone is injured in your office space or to cover any physical damage, theft, or vandalism. If you practice from your home, your insurance company needs to be aware of this so as not to void your policy.

Work space: At home or the office

If you see clients professionally, it is better to separate your workspace from your living space. Some people can arrange their home in such a way that the workspace is separate from the living space, for example in a converted garage, basement, or a room near the entrance where a washroom and waiting area are accessible and the clients are not in the personal or family space.

If this is not possible, it is not recommended to work from home. It becomes difficult to keep healthy boundaries between you and your client in your intimate space. The energies from home and work may not always be compatible. You may never feel really at home in your space because you may prioritize the arrangement and cleanliness for your clients rather than for your own comfort.

The ideal office space is completely separate from your home, either private or shared with other practitioners. You can arrange the space to your liking and not have to rearrange it when you leave. You can set up an altar where you keep sacred objects. Then the energy will build up as the space is used and becomes infused with healing energies and the presence of spiritual beings and guides that come in and assist.

With an office that is separate from your living space, it is easier to leave your preoccupations behind and be present with your clients. When you leave your office, it will also be easier to disconnect from your clients and be present with the persons who share your living space.

How much are you worth?

How much should you charge for your services? How much do you value yourself? These issues are a work in progress that is continually evolving.

When you are new to this kind of practice, you need to attract new clients. You might be afraid that if you charge the "going rate" clients will expect too much or that they might be disappointed because of your lack of experience. Or perhaps you expect too much of yourself. This is a struggle for most new practitioners.

If you have taken the time to register with a Reiki association and completed the requirements, you will have had several hours of practice. The Canadian Reiki Association, of which I am a member, requires twenty-four hours of practice before registering student members as practitioners. These practice clients can then become your first clients and they may be able to refer people to you.

I suggest that you research the price of treatments from established Reiki practitioners and other comparable techniques, such as massage, and set your price close to this amount.

As a temporary measure, you might offer the first treatment for free or at a substantial discount to attract clients, establish your practice, and help build your clientele. You can gradually increase your fee as you gain confidence and experience.

When I started my practice, I set my price significantly lower than the going rate. It took me several years to increase the price to what I now feel represents the real value for my services. Now, I would rather have fewer clients at a price I am comfortable with rather than work more for a lesser fee.

Take the risk of setting a price slightly above what you think you are worth right from the beginning and adjust it from there as time goes by.

Time boundaries

If you do all the positions of the standard protocol for the recommended three minutes, the treatment will take about forty-five minutes. You will also need some time at the beginning to find out what is needed, and at the end to debrief after the treatment, take the payment and set up another appointment. All this could easily take seventy-five minutes, depending on your personal approach. For new clients, it is wise to allow a little extra time to do the intake and introduce them to Reiki; also, keep in mind that your clients may arrive late on their first appointment if they have trouble finding your office or a place to park.

Once you have set the time frame for the session, managing it may be a challenge. This is a learning curve and you will be better able to manage it as time goes by. It helps if you clearly define the time frame at the first session and are firm, but gentle, in ending the session.

Some clients tend to stretch the time in a variety of ways for reasons that are sometimes unconscious. This can take the form of bringing things up or getting emotional in the last few minutes, asking questions once you have completed or by chatting on their way out. They may not even be aware of this dynamic, and naming it will bring it into consciousness. If it is happening with you, it is probably occurring in other areas of their lives; they would benefit from working on the issue with a therapist.

By keeping good time boundaries with your clients, you will be modeling for them how to do it for themselves.

Setting your work days and hours

Another issue I faced as I opened up my practice was how to manage the time between seeing clients and all the administrative duties that come with operating a business, including managing, accounting, continuous education, creating and organizing courses and workshops, and marketing and networking, while still keeping time for family and self-care.

I had an office that was available seven days a week and made myself available whenever a client needed me. I was afraid to say no to clients for fear that I would lose them if I were not available. I often worked evenings and weekends and it became very difficult to plan any structured time for these other important aspects of my personal and professional life. I had no boss, but not much free time either.

It was a great relief when I finally found the courage to work a limited number of hours per day and only certain days during the week. A good balance for me was seeing clients three days per week and keeping two days for administration and self-care, considering that I often taught on weekends. I found that clients readily accepted the time slots that I offered them. I was then able to lower my office rental costs by renting the space to other practitioners. It was a win-win situation.

I set aside a certain number of weekends during the year for my various workshops and courses and planned them far in advance so I could list them on my website. This way, I could plan for family and leisure activities ahead of time, and this was much more equitable for everyone.

As you experiment with your own needs, you will find what works for you.

Friends and relatives as clients?

A common question is whether to work with friends and relatives as clients. Working with friends and relatives can be beneficial, but it may not be easy due to all the underlying, and perhaps unconscious, dynamics. When you work with them you shift into a therapist role and your relationship with them may begin to change. You may find that you need to take some distance in order to remain objective.

118

It is fine to exchange with family and friends from time to time as long as there is a clear understanding that it is not a therapeutic relationship, but rather an occasional exchange of services.

At some point, you may need to decide whether you want this person as a friend or a client.

Client files and forms

As you set up your practice, you will need to set up files and various forms. Sample forms can be found on the Internet or may be available from your Reiki association.

Client record

It is useful to take a few notes on what came up during the session so you can keep track of what was worked with and follow up at the next session if necessary. Also note any changes they report on their medical condition or medications.

You can review these prior to meeting the client in case the client brings anything up from the previous session. However, it is important to simply be present with whatever the client comes in with and not bias the session with your thoughts and questions. From time to time, you may want to check all your notes and review progress since the beginning of the work together. Clients are often surprised at how much they have changed but have not noticed until you have reflected it to them.

Client intake form

A client intake form will save time at the first session and give you a chance to get to know the client ahead of time. Filling out the form helps clients reflect on why they are coming as they review their physical and emotional health history, and this actually starts the healing process. When the client arrives, she or he is already in the process and will benefit more from the treatment. If they are comfortable with it, I have my clients fill out a rather exhaustive intake form directly on my website, which is then sent automatically upon completion to a secure site from which I can download it. If they are reluctant to fill out personal information on the Internet, they can print out the form, fill it out manually, and bring it in with them.

Consent form

It is recommended to have a consent form signed by clients to keep in your file. Parents should sign the consent form for minors. A web search will yield many examples to choose from.

Supervision

Generally, the Universe will send you clients with whom you will have no difficulty working, but it will also keep you on the edge of your growth. Just as they will benefit from your presence and care, you will learn a lot from them. As you develop your practice and your ability to be with clients, there will be times when you will be challenged and triggered by them.

We are practically always reacting to the present from past experience. When the client transfers onto the practitioner this is called transference, and when the practitioner transfers onto the client it is called counter-transference.

It is important to be aware of this because if it is unconscious in you the practitioner, a client may come in who unconsciously reminds you of your mother or father and you will react to the client as if he or she were one of them. This will not be in your client's best interest. However, if you are aware of this counter-transference, you can use the Witness to respond rather than react. Sometimes counter-transference is useful for the client when it is identified and named; if it comes up between the practitioner and client, it most likely comes up in everyday life, and through it being named, they learn to recognize it and also make another choice.

A Reiki practitioner is not a psychotherapist, but being aware of these issues will positively impact relationships with clients.

Having resource persons with whom you can get curious about and explore the issues that come up between you and your clients will be very supportive for your growth. This is called supervision and is done with a person who is familiar with your practice and the issues that might come up. The supervisor can help you work through these issues so that you can continue to grow in conscious awareness and better serve your clients. In addition to helping you with your clients, it will help you with your life and your own relationships. Supervision can take different forms and is often limited to what comes up between you and your clients; it does not get into personal therapy. However, anything that comes up with your clients has to do with your own dynamics so, inevitably, you will be identifying things that can be worked on later with your therapist.

You can also do supervision in peer groups where practitioners share experiences and challenges and help each other bring clarity to the issues.

Having a supervisor and a therapist will support your growth and your practice. We all have blind spots that prevent us from seeing our personal dynamics and so it is difficult, if not impossible, to work through them without assistance.

Coaching and mentoring

Having a mentor can help you grow as a practitioner. Mentorship can take different forms, such as periodic review sessions or direct coaching while you treat a client. Your mentor could be your Reiki Master or some other person for whom you have a lot of respect in regards to the way they teach or work with clients.

A personal coach will help you define your objectives and short- and long-term goals and then help you define the steps to manifest them. Coaches have efficient exercises to help you find your passion and mission statement. Often they will offer a complimentary session so you can get to know them and decide if the chemistry between the two of you and their approach is suitable.

Molly, a colleague and a friend, and I benefited significantly from our respective skills when we exchanged regular coaching and treatment sessions for a year.

License to practice and to touch

Some jurisdictions require a license to practice Reiki and/or to lay hands on someone. Some only require that a practitioner register with the local authorities and others have no restrictions whatsoever on practicing or touching.

Check with your local jurisdiction and your Reiki association for assistance in determining what is necessary so that you can practice legally.

Internet and social media

Website

One of the first things I did when I decided to open up a practice was to set up a website. This was a worthwhile investment as it gave me an opportunity to get clear on my practice and to be found by Internet search engines from the very beginning of my practice. Over the years, as I added more and more content and approaches, popular search engines such as Google and Yahoo would list me at or very near the top of web searches made by potential clients.

I currently get about 60 to 65% of my clients and most of my students through my website.

You will probably want to set up your own website to increase your visibility and let clients know what skills you have to offer. As you develop your website, you will need to identify and get clear about what it is you want others to know about you. This in itself is a valuable exercise and a process, and it will help you define your unique self as a practitioner.

You can find websites on the Internet that will help you build websites. Some of them are free and others are inexpensive and very good. Eventually, you will probably want to hire someone to do it professionally. There are a lot of things to consider in order to ensure that your website is search engine friendly. Choose a web designer who is knowledgeable and can set this up for you.

Blogs

Blogs are an effective way to share your views and invite interaction from readers. It is easy to set up a blog on the Internet that can be linked to your website.

Social media

Social media, such as Facebook, Twitter, and others, is becoming a very popular and effective way to promote a professional practice.

Some marketing tips

I am not a marketing expert, but here are some of the other things that I have done or currently do to promote myself in addition to setting up my website.

<u>Networking</u>

For several years, I was a member of BNI (Business Network International, <www.bni.com>). This is a networking referral club that meets weekly. It is extremely well structured and efficient. It teaches you about networking and how to promote yourself and gives you the opportunity to meet many people who you would not otherwise meet. Costs include the membership fee in addition to that of the weekly breakfasts. Some time is required outside of the weekly meetings to get to know the other members and to invite guests to the weekly meetings. The focus is on referring each other's services when it is beneficial for clients. I have met some really great people there and still do business with them years after leaving the club—my web designer, financial advisor, independent car salesman, real estate agents, chiropractor, massage therapists, and other colleagues are all people who I met through BNI.

It is a great opportunity to introduce Reiki to people who would not otherwise find out about it. As an example, one of the members shopping at a health food store saw a notice that the storeowners were looking for a Reiki Master. I followed up on her referral, and found out that they organized free round table presentations on a weekly basis to draw in customers. I eventually gave a talk there on Reiki and had eight people attend, three of which became Reiki students.

Networking is fun and one of most effective ways to build a clientele and resources.

Seminars and talks

Giving free lectures or short introductions to Reiki whenever you can at healing schools, community centers, and other organizations will give you exposure and spread the word. For the last few years, I have had the honor of presenting Reiki to fourth-year medical students at McGill University in Montreal, Canada.

Pamphlets and business cards

These are necessary to have in your practice. Preparing them will help you to define your practice and the services you offer.

I distribute my pamphlets and business cards to several local outlets, and once I am known there, I just mail them the pamphlets with a note saying "Thank you for posting." This saves a lot of time and expense. I visit occasionally to check if they have put up what I sent them and nourish the relationship with them.

Paid advertising

I have my business cards and pamphlets at a few outlets where I pay a small sum ($100/yr.) to have it displayed in an individual slot. These types of display areas are managed, exclusive to subscribers, clean, well organized, and thus very effective. Some of the outlets will call when they are out of material so I can send them more.

I occasionally advertise in community directories that are distributed to up to 40,000 homes in the neighborhood where I have my office. Even though most people probably only look at these when they get it and then put it aside, I did get a long-term client from one $150 listing, and so it was a worthwhile investment.

I advertise in health magazines with a large circulation and then monitor the results. I advertised consistently in one magazine for several years until it went out of business a few years ago. I still meet people today who remember me from that magazine; some had kept the ad and eventually contacted me years later.

In advertising, two key factors for success are repetition and consistency.

Newsletters

I contact professional organizations to distribute any pertinent information to their members in their emails or newsletters if they will allow it. Sometimes, this is free and other times there is a minimal cost.

Web advertising

I am listed on several websites, some paid, some not.

Some of the paid websites I use are:

- o <Byregion.net >
- o <Alternativesante.com>

I occasionally do a search for Reiki organizations and web pages. Some of them offer free listings on their practitioner directories. This is especially efficient for the ones that come up at the top of the search inquiries.

Some of the free ones I have found include:

- o <www.BodyMindSpiritDirectory.org>
- o <www.thereikipage.com>

An interesting phenomenon is that I get listed at no cost on websites I have never visited by individuals and organizations that have liked what they found on my website.

I occasionally do a search on myself just to see how many pages come up where I am referenced and am usually surprised at the results.

Reiki associations

I am a member and registered teacher with the Canadian Reiki Association, which costs about $100/yr. and gives me visibility and credibility. Their web directory listing includes a short bio and a link to my website.

Your own newsletter and mailing list

You can put out a periodic newsletter of your activities and other pertinent information for members who sign up for your mailing list. This can keep you visible and is an efficient way to stay in touch with clients and promote your practice and any workshops you put together. You can ask clients when they fill out the intake form if they wish to be on your general mailing list.

I eventually had to find a better way to manage my mailing list. A friend introduced me to MailChimp, a fabulous service for creating professional newsletters and automatically managing mailing lists, to which clients can subscribe to or unsubscribe from without any input from me. This service is currently free for a maximum of 2,000 members per day and 12,000 emails per month. MailChimp is one of many such services available on the web. TargetHero is another that is completely free.

Free giveaways of useful information

I received an email a few years ago about writing out Abundance Checks on a monthly basis as a way of letting the Universe know I was ready to receive. I loved the idea and decided to put it on my website to make it available to everyone. I send out a monthly reminder to my mailing list.

This is very popular and gets circulated to friends and acquaintances. Many new people sign up each month for the reminders, and some even sign up for my general emails on my activities and workshops. At the very least, my website gets a lot of visits from friends of clients. You can check it out for yourself and sign up for the monthly reminders.

Referral incentive

I hesitated for a long time before doing this because I was afraid that my clients would refer me for the wrong reasons. Recently, I have decided to give a substantial rebate each time I get a referral from a client.

My experience has been that my clients really appreciate this. Many times, my thank-you email is synchronistic because they had already been thinking about returning; the thank-you email provides the incentive to book a session.

Package discounts

At the same time as I initiated the referral incentive, I began to offer a substantial discount for clients who paid up front for four or six sessions. This has the advantage of getting a commitment from the client for ongoing treatments, filling my agenda in advance, and, more importantly, giving the client a real chance to experience the benefits of treatments over a period of time rather than coming in for only one treatment. Often they will continue to come periodically after these initial treatments.

Trade shows and expos

You can set up a booth in a trade show and health expos where you can introduce yourself and meet other professionals doing Reiki or practicing other approaches. These are usually well attended and worth the time and effort.

If cost is an issue, you can share a booth with another person or participate in one sponsored by your association.

<u>Your turn</u>

I am sure that you can come up with many other ideas to promote yourself. Taking a marketing course in your community will be well worth the time and resources you invest.

Reiki in your environment

In your community

As Reiki gets more popular, it is being introduced into community centers, resource centers, senior residences, and other places. These centers need volunteers to give treatments. If there are none in your community, you might think about setting something up. Your Reiki association may be able to help you with this.

With other health professionals

As you network and get to know other health professionals, they will undoubtedly get curious about what you do. Some may even be interested in exchanging treatments so they can be in a position to refer you when it is appropriate.

In schools and colleges

Some schools and colleges have begun to offer Reiki in their curriculum for interested students.

Reiki in hospitals

Many hospitals are introducing Reiki as a paid or free service as they become aware of the many benefits for patients before, during, and after medical interventions.

Dr. Mehmet Oz often invites a Reiki Master into the operating room while performing surgery. The Reiki practitioner is doing a treatment at the same time as the surgeon is operating to help support the client during the process. See this YouTube video on Dr. Oz's viewpoint on Energy Medicine and the use of Reiki Masters for heart patients:
<www.youtube.com/watch?v=HJ5eajLCzu0&feature=player _embedded.>

Julie Motz reported some of the results from his studies in *Hands of Life* (Motz, 1998).

William Rand of the International Center for Reiki Training has done a lot to promote and document Reiki in hospitals as well as coordinate research on the benefits of Reiki.

Summary of Chapter 5

Some of the people initiated into Reiki will practice professionally. Others will limit their practice to self, family, and friends. All them will integrate Reiki into their daily lives and their workplace from their creativity and their passion.

For those who choose to practice Reiki professionally, it is strongly advised to take an ethics course. Each new Reiki practitioner will have to decide whether to work at home or in an office. The practice then becomes a business to be administered, whether it is small or large. In addition to all the administrative tasks that come with a practice and a business, marketing will be necessary in order to build and maintain a clientele. Time management and boundaries follow a learning curve, and there are many tools available to support the practitioner in this endeavor.

Supervision, coaching, and mentoring become important to support the practitioner's growth in order to best serve the client.

Besides a personal and professional Reiki practice, the practitioner can contribute to spreading Reiki in the community and in hospitals as conventional medicine becomes more and more familiar with this gentle and beneficial method.

CHAPTER 6

TRANSFORMATION THROUGH REIKI

In this chapter, I would like to expand on the personal growth and transformation that Reiki offers and for which it is a catalyst.

The healing journey

I often describe the healing path as a generally upward incline with dips and valleys leading to more and more stable higher ground. As we move forward on this path, we discover our deep early wounding, and the resulting images and limiting beliefs we have created which organize our present moment experience and often prevent us from taking in nourishment even though it might be available.

We might also discover the masks we hide behind or need to wear in order to protect our vulnerability when reality becomes too frightening. We might shed light on our shadow, those parts of us that we dislike and hold out of the light so we don't have to see them. We may come face to face with the idealized self-image that we try to live up to but that is ever impossible to achieve. We may come to know the dynamics we use to defend and protect ourselves.

It is unbelievable how much energy we expend in trying to uphold all these ways to survive. This is energy we withhold from life and that prevents us from living and enjoying fully.

As we develop the Witness or Observer Self, and accept that we are responsible for our experience, we start to transform and grow in self-love and love for others. Inadvertently, the dynamics and images and beliefs resurface;

we occasionally regress to an earlier state of being. It feels as if we are taking one step forward and two steps back.

The good news is that as we risk trying on new possibilities, we have some positive reinforcing experiences. These become reference points that we can return to in difficult times. Even though it can get very intense, we spend less time in these old dynamics and states of being.

Reiki will open up your energy field and act as a catalyst for doorways to appear that you may not have seen before. Synchronicities will begin to happen which will lead you to new experiences and people on your path that will offer possibilities for new learning and growth. This is simply the Universe responding to your soul's plan that led you to take the course.

Spirituality on the path

The word spirituality often scares people in our Western culture because of the negative experience many have had with religion or because they do not understand it. A person can be religious without being spiritual and spiritual without being religious; one does not necessarily follow the other.

So what does being spiritual mean?

The word spirituality contains the word "spirit." Being spiritual simply means being in touch with spirit. Our Western culture idolizes the body, material consumption, and doing and often judges or belittles being, introspection, and anything to do with emotions and spirit. We all have a spirit, a soul, whether or not we believe in an afterlife. Without the presence of the life force and vital energy, the body dies.

The more you are in touch with your spirit, the more you become aware of who you really are and the more you are able to give a deeper meaning to your life. My son Benoit, at sixteen years old, told us that he wanted to walk about fifty kilometers to a local mountain that is an energy vortex and holds a high vibration. As parents, we were a little (a lot?) concerned about him venturing out alone at his age, but we decided to support his initiative and let him go on this adventure. When he returned safe and sound three days later, he sat down and wrote twenty-one pages reflecting on his experience. This sentence stood out for me and still resonates:

"The meaning of life is to give your life meaning."

Reiki will stimulate deeper contact with yourself and your life task and your spirituality. As you come more into contact with yourself, you may start to feel more in touch and connected with all that is around you, the Universe, and the Greater Whole.

Growth of the Reiki practitioner

As a Reiki practitioner, you will move along this path at your own pace as the Reiki energy you channel for yourself and others begins to clear your energy field.

So much has transpired for me since I took my first Reiki course in 1994. My Reiki practice has evolved into an integration of several approaches that I apply depending on the need of the client in the moment. Little did I know where this simple weekend course was going to take me!

Here is Reiki Master Dimitra's experience:

Reiki benefits my body, mind, soul, and environment.

Reiki transforms me each time. After each session, my external world may remain the same but my vision becomes different. I am happy and in a state of bliss simply because I am.

Reiki teaches me to let go of attachments, expectations, and answers.

Reiki allows me to experience the perfection of Oneness in the Universe.

Reiki instills peace, love, joy, passion, safety within, and the faith that all is perfect as is.

Reiki heals so that my True Self can reveal itself.

Roland, thank you so much for your guidance, kindness, and generosity that gave me the courage to take my practice to another level.

Forever Grateful, -

Dimitra Panaritis, Montreal

Developing the Witness

The most important and indispensable skill that you can develop to help and support you along your journey is the Witness, that part of you that can observe, without judgment, with compassion and curiosity, what you are doing, how you are doing it, and what emotions are present. The more you develop the Witness, the more you will become conscious of yourself and your dynamics. The first step in healing is to become aware and shed light on what was in shadow. Once there is light, that part of you can never go back into shadow. I highly recommend *The Dark Side of the Light Chasers* (Ford 1998). In this book, Debbie Ford helps readers become conscious of how things that trigger them in other people are actually something they don't like in themselves.

As you work with and hone the Witness, you will gradually begin to respond to situations and people instead of reacting automatically. When you first start to develop this skill, you may utilize the Witness after the fact, perhaps later in the day or the next day. As you become more adept, you will begin to use it in the moment and "see and watch" yourself as you react in the same way over and over again. Eventually, you will choose to hit the pause button and take the time to respond rather than react. Then things will begin to change, because you will be making conscious choices aligned with your true nature and begin to take responsibility for what happens and what you create in your life. Developing self-responsibility does not mean that you start to blame yourself and feel guilty for what happens. It means that you are now acting from choice and taking your power back instead of being a victim of circumstances and the people with whom you interact. This is very freeing.

Ongoing support for self-improvement

As you move along the journey, you will encounter resources in the form of teachers and colleagues who will assist you. Effective therapy is very helpful in moving your process along. It is difficult, if not impossible, to do this journey alone no matter how well you learn things by yourself. We all have our blind spots and, by definition, we cannot be conscious of something that we are unconscious of.

After my first Reiki course, I became aware that I needed to do something about the way I was being with my children. I had had a difficult childhood with a father who loved me very much but from whom I experienced a lot of verbal abuse and anger. I was being the same with my young children. I found someone to help me look at my story. The relationship with my sons and my spouse started to change for the better as I began to take responsibility and move away from being the victim. Today, it is completely different as I respond (most of the time anyways) rather than react to my experience!

It was mandatory to have therapy support during the six years I attended the Barbara Brennan School of Healing and it is required for my current training in Core Energetics. This provides ongoing support to be with whatever comes up for me in my own process during the intense trainings and the subsequent effect on my life and relationships as I integrate the work. I find this kind of support invaluable for anyone who is accompanying clients on their healing journey. I continue to see my therapist even when it is not required during training. We cannot take anyone where we have not gone ourselves. The deeper we go into our own issues, the more we can be with ourselves and the more we can be with others.

In Appendix G, I have listed and briefly described some of the effective therapies I have experienced, trained in, or with which I am otherwise familiar.

Health and self-care

You may find as you continue down this path that your needs begin to change, as does your focus on health issues. Let your body and your intuition be your guide on this road and show you what you need to do to feel better and strengthen your energetic container.

Here are some of the ways this self-care has evolved for me:

As I continued to work energetically with clients, teach, and organize various workshops, I felt I needed to clear my container to become a more powerful channel for the energy.

I have, for the last 30+ years, had a morning exercise routine to take care of my physical body—a bit of yoga, some push-ups, and various other exercises that change depending on my current needs, discoveries, and experimentations. Lately, I have felt the need to add a meditation to this routine.

About ten years ago, I became interested in nutrition and started to take supplements to make sure I had all the antioxidants and trace minerals that I could not get from the food I was eating.

Lately, I have started to eat a high percentage of raw and organic food in order to maximize the intake of enzymes and minimize the food additives, and although I still eat seafood, I've gotten away from eating white and red meat. In addition to positively contributing environmentally in this way, my body expends less energy breaking down and rebuilding the proteins that are found in meat. I have found more compatible and efficient sources of protein. My tolerance to alcohol is greatly reduced as time goes by and I consume much less.

I get additional support from complementary approaches, such as massage, energy healing, fasciatherapy, chiropractic, acupuncture, osteopathy, and others.

Continuous education

It is very likely, even if it is not necessary, that as you read about Reiki, work with clients, and meet other practitioners who work in alternative and complementary medicine, you will be drawn to courses and seminars to expand your skills. There are so many interesting approaches out there that can complement the work that you do as a Reiki practitioner. Some associations actually require members to do a minimum amount of continuing education.

Prior to learning Reiki, I read about one book per year; I would often read before bed and fall asleep after reading just a few pages. Since I have discovered Reiki and studied many other techniques, I am amazed at the number of books I read and how fascinated I am by them.

It was while talking about chakras during my first Reiki course that my friend John brought in *Hands of Light* (Brennan, 1988). Six months later, I was enrolled in the school and have since been drawn to many other trainings to supplement my skills as a healing facilitator and therapist.

Clearing and strengthening your channel

The Reiki energy comes through the crown chakra and goes to the heart and into your hands. Other energy frequencies are drawn through all your chakras from the universal energy field, including the low frequency grounding energies from the root or first chakra. All these are made available to the client when you give a treatment.

As you integrate some of the above suggestions into your lifestyle, your own energy field will begin to clear. Some of the chakras that might have been habitually dysfunctional will open and remain stable. Some of the stagnant energy in your energy bodies will dissipate and your aura will generally become more harmonious. Everyone around you will notice the difference. They may say something like "You look well lately," or "Have you changed something? You seem more peaceful these days." They will want to be around you more—you will attract different people who will resonate with your new vibrations.

As your energy field clears, these energies will come through more easily and be available for the client. I like to use the image of a vacuum cleaner filter that reduces the flow of air when it is clogged with dust. The air flows much more easily when it has been cleaned. You will be able to run more energy as you give treatments because your field will be less resistant to the flow of energy.

Your clients will definitely feel the difference in your treatments.

Unfolding of the Reiki Master/Teacher

"You teach best what you most need to learn" (Bach, 1977)

Even though I carry the title of Reiki Master, I've always considered myself more of a teacher than a master of Reiki. The word master conjures up for me total control and complete knowledge of the art. While I am able to transmit the teachings and have gained a lot of experience, I am always learning and I don't believe I have yet, or ever will, master the art.

You may have wanted to become a Reiki Master from the very beginning or feel the desire to pass this on as you integrate the teachings and continue to practice.

Becoming a Reiki Master is a commitment to yourself first, then to others.

At the master level, it is about integrating Reiki such that when it is passed on to students, the teaching originates primarily from the heart rather than from the mind. It is more than teaching others techniques and hand positions; it is about sacred transmission of the integrated learning of the path, the principles, and the journey of self-discovery that Reiki offers. As a Reiki Master, you undertake the responsibility of accompanying students along the path and selecting candidates for the master level. It is about assisting your students to discover themselves and their abilities and grow with the principles, so that they can in turn teach and assist students.

Being a Reiki Master means being available for your students in between classes as they move through their process and any associated issues. It means being available to organize and lead Reiki Shares to give them a chance to practice and continue learning.

As a Reiki Master, you will need to get yourself out of the way so that you can be a clear and pure instrument for your students' highest good. This means putting the immature ego aside; this can be a humbling experience at times. In order to do this, you will have to get to know yourself a whole lot better.

You will need to keep the same healthy boundaries with students as you do with clients. This means not being friends with them but accompanying them on their path. They need to have the space for their process and learning without having to take care of the relationship between you and them. There may be times when they will react to you as their Teacher/Master and you will need to be totally there for them in unconditional presence as they move through their process. And they may need your support from time to time as they build their practice and begin teaching.

As the common saying goes, "The journey is more important than the destination." Reiki is a journey unto one's self, along which we are able to assist others. It is of utmost importance for you not to rush through the various levels. The apprenticeship to become a Reiki Master with Usui, and also with Takata, was a long process and a lifetime commitment. The tendency in our Western society has been to shorten the time and rush through the process. For some, it is more of an ego trip to accumulate another title or diploma.

Take your time finding the right person to accompany you on this path. You may elect to do all your training with the same Reiki Master or decide along the way to experience the teachings of several. It is possible that the person you choose will trigger your process and this may be a good thing if it helps you grow. Before you decide to change because you have been triggered, I encourage you to examine your motives and discuss them with your Reiki Master if that is possible. Doing so may help you to get clear on some of the issues that have come up and allow you to get beyond them. Your Reiki Master will be able to coach you in this process and hold the intention for your highest good; if it seems appropriate for you to change, he or she will more than likely encourage you to do so. Any untoward resistance on the part of the Reiki Master for you to change may be an indication that change might just be the right decision for you.

Once you have found a person with whom you feel comfortable, get plenty of exposure to teaching by attending Reiki classes as an observer/assistant. This will allow you to integrate the teaching at a much deeper level. All that you learn you will integrate into your own unique way of teaching.

Being able to contribute as a Reiki Master is a very nourishing and enriching experience, and I encourage you to pursue this path if you are drawn to it.

Becoming the master of your life

Regardless of whether you stick with the first level of Reiki or go on to become a Reiki Master, there is no doubt in my mind that Reiki will help you to become the master of your life. To me, this means growing in consciousness and self-awareness, being in contact with the self, listening to the voices of your own true nature, living in the present moment, and making choices aligned with your true nature and life mission. It means taking full responsibility for everything that happens in your life.

This is a lifelong journey, and probably one of many lifetimes.

Summary of Chapter 6

Reiki is a catalyst and helps to align to one's life mission and spirituality. Personal growth takes on more importance and doors open wide to support this growth and to place people, resources, and tools on the path.

This growth will touch all aspects of life: personal growth, consciousness, work, health, nutrition, and professional development to expand knowledge and skills. All these bring the practitioner closer to him or herself and help to better serve the client. As time goes on, the energy field clears and becomes more harmonious: an even more powerful channel for the healing energy.

This transformation continues through all the levels and allows the inner master to emerge.

At the master level, the practitioner can humbly transmit these sacred teachings to those who come towards him. The Master is in service of life and consciousness and of all those who desire to let their own Master emerge.

This inner transformation does not stop at the level of Master/Teacher. Growth and conscious awareness are a life-long journey, perhaps spanning many lifetimes.

IN SUMMARY

Reiki, a powerful catalyst for personal transformation and healing—this has been the main theme of this book.

The initiation received during the course is the main catalyst; it augments the capacity to channel the Reiki energy and increases the level of vibration of the energy field.

Reiki, as a catalyst, aligns the initiate to his or her life mission and spirituality. Personal growth takes on more importance and the road opens wide through synchronicities that place people, resources, and tools on the path of the practitioner.

As time goes by, the energy field clears and becomes more harmonious: an even more powerful channel for the healing energy. The transformation continues through the levels and allows the inner Master to emerge and the initiate to accomplish his or her life mission.

Reiki, created by Mikao Usui after his discoveries in the ancient Tibetan sutras, is simple and easy to learn and apply. It is accessible to all and can act on all levels—physical, emotional, mental, psychic, and spiritual.

The five principles guide the Reiki practitioner, and the additional principle of exchange encourages the active participation of the receiver on the healing journey as well as ensuring a balance between the giver and the receiver.

Reiki, which is transmitted through the energy field by laying hands on the body, can be used on oneself, other people, animals, plants, food, objects, and situations. It can be sent at a distance and can act in the present, past, and future.

Reiki is complementary to conventional medicine and is neither a cure nor a guarantee that healing will take place.

The practitioner does not diagnose medical conditions nor prescribes medication.

Traditional Reiki is learned in three or four levels depending on the lineage of the Master/Teacher.

It is important to realize that a person giving Reiki can take on the role of therapist and to better serve the clients, the practitioner must be conscious of what this might represent. The preparation, ambiance, touch, equipment, and accessories all have a positive effect on the session and can ensure maximum efficiency of the treatment.

The relationship between the practitioner and the client is one of the most important factors in the treatment, much more so than any specific technique. The presence of the practitioner plays a crucial role in this relationship.

The more the practitioner works to clear his or her channel, the more powerful the treatments become. This requires a commitment to the self, to the clients and students should he or she eventually choose to transmit these sacred teachings to those who put him on their path.

CLOSING WORDS

As I wrote this book, I constantly struggled with the question that was asked after I posted a request for testimonials on a Reiki Facebook page: "Does the world really need another book on Reiki?" There are so many good books out there (some of my favorites are listed in Appendix D) that I wondered if mine would make a difference.

In order to get this writing project off the ground, I knew I had to take some time off and get away from everyday life and all its preoccupations. I chose to go to Indonesia, one of the most exotic places I had visited in my previous travels. This was a wonderful adventure and a holiday at the same time. The Santai Beach Inn in Sengiggi, Lombok was the perfect place—quiet, by the ocean, always sunny and warm and blessed with a truly wonderful and hospitable staff. It turned out to be a very prolific place to write. I wrote most of the book in the month I spent here in Lombok, Indonesia, the island just east of Bali.

As I began to share my knowledge and experience in this idyllic setting while continually connected to the Reiki energies, I was able to find the answer to my question.

In the book, I have shared many of my own experiences and viewpoints on the various aspects of Reiki. It felt wonderful just to be able to present my approach to teaching and applying Reiki and express the love and respect I have for it.

But I really tapped into my passion and how nourishing the whole experience of Reiki is when I began to reread, select, and include the testimonials that I received from some of my clients and the novice students, practitioners, and Reiki Masters I have trained.

These testimonials are the reason I continue to teach and practice, and they fuel my passion for self-improvement. It moves me deeply to witness how this simple method of hands-on healing is transformative.

This book adds very little to the vast knowledge and experience that is already available on Reiki. Yet, it is my own small and unique contribution to Reiki that has emerged from my essence and my gift. Perhaps the entire book, or just one testimonial, will pique your curiosity enough to try it out by getting a treatment or taking the first level course. Perhaps my book will enrich and influence the practice of a few students and practitioners as well as the practice and teaching style of some Reiki Masters.

That will be reason enough for me to have written the book.

I am writing this book in the year 2012, the end of the Mayan calendar and a year that is prophesized to be one of enormous change, the tipping point for a quantum leap in consciousness for humanity. The Earth is already showing us signs of this upheaval with the earthquakes, such as the ones in Haiti and Japan, the floods, and upsets in meteorological conditions—heavy rains, record temperatures, fires, tsunamis, and heat waves. Our financial and social systems are showing signs of major transformation and even collapse. The US dollar is faltering, the Euro is fragile, and there are major upsets in governments in Egypt, Libya, Syria, Tunisia, the Arab World, and elsewhere.

Young people around the world are getting involved and uniting to question social values and our materialistic society, making way for major changes in consciousness. Movements such as Occupy Wall Street have an influence on the way the democratic world is governed. Indigo and Crystal children, born with a higher consciousness, are influencing the adults around them by their way of perceiving and being in the world. I hear many testimonials from parents who are amazed at the questions, comments, and teachings that their very young children come up with.

As I witness these world events, it seems that suffering, strife, and war are ever on the increase. Yet I see and feel a shift in consciousness; more and more people, and younger people, are drawn to alternative and complementary approaches and spirituality, including Reiki. They are questioning their values and their way of life. I am confident that we will tip the balance and create a world that will be much more equal and harmonious in the years to come. I am also of the opinion that this will happen without undue cataclysm and suffering.

This will require a dedication to ourselves, humanity, and our Earth as well as the willingness to embrace change despite underlying fear and insecurity. We will need to surrender to a Higher Knowing and trust that we can create it.

Whether you like it or not, you have chosen to be here in this time with the seven billion other souls who came to take part in this momentous time in our evolution. You can influence what happens, you can make a difference; that is why you are here. Which way will you choose? What do you wish to create? What is the gift you have brought to share? Are you willing to let go of being the victim and take full responsibility for what you have and are creating in each moment?

These are tough questions and tough choices. I have faith that you and the rest of humanity will listen to and follow inner guidance and find the right answers.

I would like to end with this text from *A Return to Love* (Williamson, 1992) that I have posted on my bathroom wall.

149

Our deepest fear is not that we are inadequate. Our deepest fear is that we are powerful beyond measure. It is our light, not our darkness that most frightens us. We ask ourselves, "Who am I to be brilliant, gorgeous, talented, fabulous?" Actually, who are you not to be? You are a child of God. Your playing small does not serve the world. There is nothing enlightened about shrinking so that other people won't feel insecure around you. We are all meant to shine, as children do. We were born to make manifest the glory of God that is within us. It's not just in some of us; it's in everyone. And as we let our own light shine, we unconsciously give other people permission to do the same. As we are liberated from our own fear, our presence automatically liberates others. (p. 190 – reprinted with permission)

May you be inspired to embrace your Light, may you allow the Master to emerge and radiate your Light so that others can see themselves in it. May you accomplish all the life tasks and spread all the gifts you came to share in this incarnation.

May you give yourself the precious gift that is Reiki. Even if you never intend to give treatments, the catalyst it will be in your life will make it a truly worthwhile and rich experience that you will absolutely not regret.

May you be happy and at peace.

May you be safe.

May you be free of suffering.

May you live in this world with well-being, abundance, and ease.

Namaste – Roland Bérard, Lombok, August 2012

WORDS OF THANKS, GRATITUDE, AND APPRECIATION

I want to thank my mother and father for giving me life, and creating the circumstances I needed to develop my capabilities as a person and a healing facilitator, and for loving me especially when I wasn't able to let it in. I now know that the early childhood wounding I experienced, unknowingly created by my parents, became the springboard for the qualities and strengths I needed to develop so I could fulfill my life mission.

I want to thank my brothers and sisters for continuous support on my strange, and somewhat estranged, life journey. My sister Louise has always believed in me and is always there to listen, understand, and support my projects. Her husband Gilles is like a brother to me; he was the first to receive distance treatments when I began to practice in 1998 during the time he was recovering from a hip replacement operation. He was also my first student.

I am forever grateful to my sons Philip and Benoit and to my former spouse Marla for their unfailing support as I went through the ups and downs of searching for my inner truth and my path. The process caused upheavals in our way of life as I left the high salaried and secure position of engineering project manager to venture out and build my practice as a healing professional, with all the uncertainty and financial worries that this entailed.

I have been blessed with many, many incredible mentors and Master teachers along the way: Bernard Grenier (formerly Chetan Aseem), my Reiki Master; Barbara Brennan and all the amazing teachers on her staff—too numerous to mention; Donna Martin, friend, teacher, and mentor of the Hakomi Method; the late Ron Kurtz, founder of the Hakomi

Method; Gary Craig (whom I have learned from on countless videos but have yet to meet) for his incredible and very generous gift to the world of the Emotional Freedom Technique (EFT); and Lorraine Desmarais, director of Coeur Énergétique, Montreal and her wonderful faculty.

Thanks also to Lorraine Desmarais, who supports and guides me through my own process and has been my therapist for many years, and to Yolaine St-Germain, my therapist during my years of training at the Barbara Brennan School of Healing.

Thanks the creators of the many healing approaches I have had the honor to study and integrate: Alexander Lowen and John Pierrakos, co-creators of Bioenergetics; John Pierrakos, creator of Core Energetics and his wife Eva Brock, creator of The Pathwork; Danis Bois, creator of Somato-PsychoPédagogie (SPP or fasciatherapy, as it was formerly called); Vianna Stibal, creator of ThetaHealing.

I want to acknowledge all the writers and contributors to modern psychology, from Freud to Reich and the subsequent authors who followed. They were sources of knowledge and inspiration on my journey, directly or indirectly through books or other venues.

I want to thank all my friends and my Biodanza group for their continuous presence, love, and support.

Thank you to my cousin June Kallestad for helping out in the editing of the first version of my book and to my sister Louise for countless hours spent reading, re-reading and editing.

Thank you to Sylvie Drolet and Dave Caldwell for volunteering to be photographed.

Thank you to those who were willing to share their experience and have their testimonials included in the book.

And I thank all my clients and students for giving me to opportunity to serve and for all the ways that they have been teachers for me and helped me grow just by being who they are.

APPENDICES

Appendix A – Reiki Treatment Positions

The Reiki positions shown on the following pages are the basic positions for giving a treatment. They are aligned with the chakras, the endocrine glands, and the major joints. These are the places on the body where the energy penetrates the easiest into the energy field.

The suggested time is three minutes per position. In the beginning, it is important to give yourself that time on all the positions so that you can learn to sense the energy.

As you gain experience and develop your senses, you will learn to sense whether you need to stay longer or not on a given position. Follow your intuition.

Once you have done all the basic positions, you can then lay your hands on the other parts of the body that need attention, either those to which you are drawn or those mentioned by the client.

Here is a summary of the positions.

Treatment Positions

Self Treatment	Treatment on others
Front	**Front**
1-Top of the head	1-Eyes
2-Eyes	2-Temples
3-Temples	3-Behind the head
4-Behind the head	4-Throat
5-Shoulders	5-Heart
6-Throat	6-Solar plexus
7-Heart	7-Sacrum (front)
8-Solar plexus	8-Root (groin)
9-Sacrum (front)	9-Knees
10-Root (groin)	10-Ankles
11-Knees	11-Underneath the feet
12-Ankles	
13-Underneath the feet	
Back	**Back**
14-Behind solar plexus	12-Behind the heart
15-Sacrum	13-Behind solar plexus
16-Coccyx	14-Sacrum
	15-Coccyx

Positions – Self Reiki

Top of the head
(7th chakra)

Eyes
(6th chakra)

Temples
(6th chakra)

Behind the head
(behind the 6th chakra)

Shoulders

Positions – Self Reiki

Throat   Throat (alternative)
(5th chakra)

Heart   Solar Plexus
4th chakra)   (3rd chakra)

Sacrum   Root (groin)
(2nd chakra)   (1st chakra)

Positions – Self Reiki

Knees

Ankles   Feet

Feet (alternative)

Positions – Self Reiki

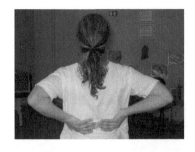
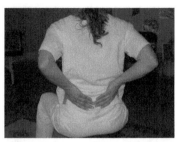

Behind the solar plexus   Sacrum

Coccyx

Positions – Other person

 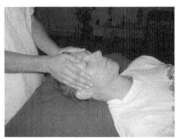

Eyes   Temples
(6th chakra)

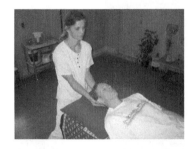 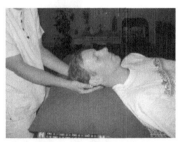

Behind the head (6th chakra)

 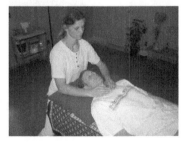

Throat (5th chakra)

Positions – Other person

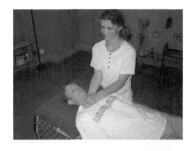 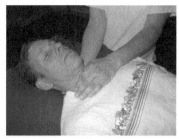

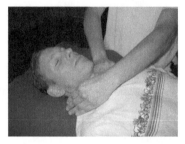

Alternative for the throat (5th chakra)

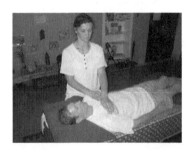 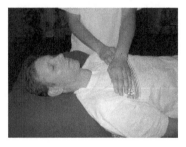

Heart (4th chakra)

Positions – Other person

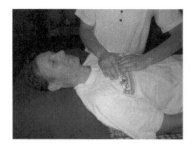 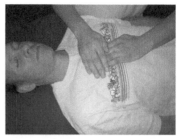

Alternative for the heart (4th chakra)

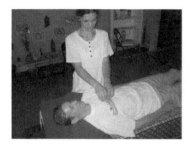 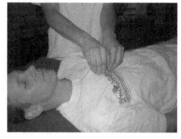

Alternative for the heart (4th chakra)

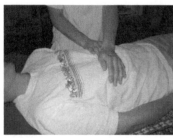 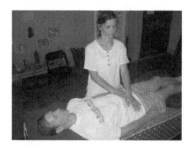

Solar plexus (3rd chakra) Sacrum (front of 2nd chakra)

Positions – Other person

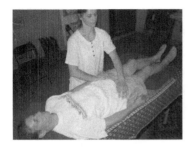
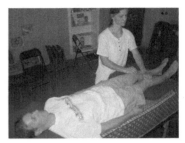

Groin (1st chakra)   Knees

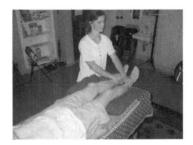

Ankles

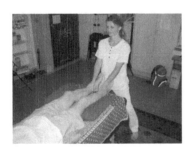

Alternative for the ankles

Positions – Other person

Feet

Feet

Alternative for the feet

Positions – Other person - Back

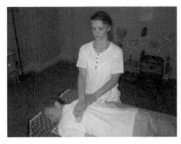 

Behind the heart (4th chakra)

Behind the solar plexus (3rd chakra)

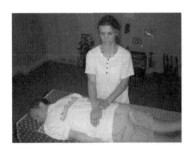 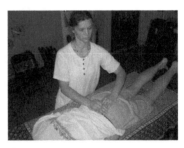

Sacrum (2nd chakra)   Coccyx (1st chakra)

Mental/Emotional Treatment

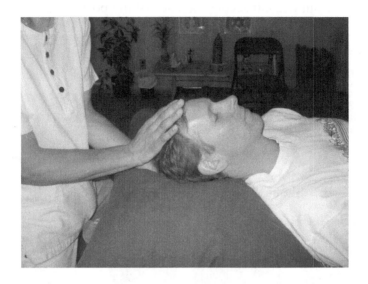

Crown

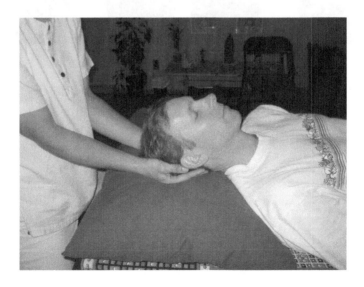

Underneath the head

Quick Treatment

Count 15-30 seconds at each of the positions.

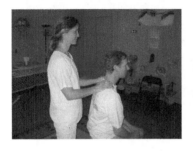
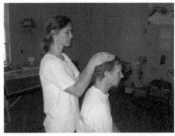

Shoulders   Crown Chakra

6th Chakra   5th Chakra

4th Chakra 3rd Chakra

2nd Chakra 1st Chakra

171

Treating Animals

This is taken from the following website which allows reproduction as long as copyright credits are noted.

Article and images copyright Patinkas © 2009-2012

<www.patinkas.co.uk/Chakra_System_of_Animals/chakra_s ystem_of_animals.html>

Please note: The information contained below is not meant as a substitute for seeking professional help if you have an animal who is sick, injured or you think may be unwell. Always seek help and advice from a qualified veterinary surgeon in the first instance.

Introduction

Animals, in common with all other living beings, have a chakra system. This system is a complex network of spinning, energy vortices (often called 'petals' in Eastern traditions) which run throughout the entire body. Universal energy (Prana, Chi, Ki) flows in and out of the chakras, along the meridian system, into the aura and then finally into the physical body. The energy flows two ways; inward and out. Therefore, every thought, act and emotion affects the chakras and is mirrored in the aura. Likewise, external stimuli, both positive and negative, have an effect on the chakras and leave their mark in the aura (including physical injuries). This is the same for animals and humans alike.

For those unfamiliar with the chakra system, if you imagine the subtle energy body (made up of chakras, linked to meridians and contained in the aura) as being like a car engine, and the physical body is the actual vehicle which the engine drives, it is not difficult to see that when the car starts to perform less effectively or even breaks down, that it's the engine which needs repairing or re-tuning and not the car's bodywork. It's the same with the subtle energy body. When we re-charge/realign the chakras (get them spinning in harmony and at the correct rate) you get the physical body running smoothly once again.

Animal Chakras

Animals have:

o   8 Major Chakras
o   21 Minor Chakras
o   6 Bud Chakras

Animals have eight Major chakras, 21 Minor chakras and six Bud chakras. Alongside the seven Major chakras that animals share with humans (Crown, Third Eye, Throat, Heart, Solar Plexus, Sacral and Root), there is another Major chakra which is unique to animals. It is called the Brachial or Key chakra. This chakra was discovered by the world's foremost and internationally renowned animal healer, Margrit Coates (click here to visit Margrit's website, The Animal Healer).

The Brachial chakra is located on either side of the body, in the area of the shoulders. It is the main energy center in all animals and links directly to all other chakras. It is the center which relates to animal-human interaction and any healing should always begin at this chakra. Animals which have a strong, healthy link with their human companions usually have a vibrant Brachial chakra, as it is the center where the animal-human bond is formed and carried.

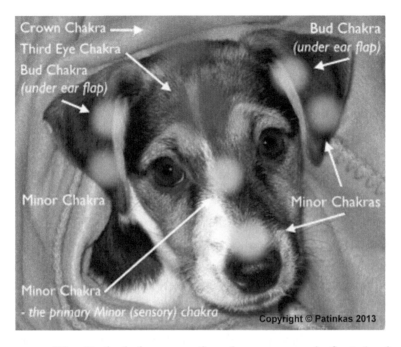

The Bud chakras are found one on each foot (pad, paw, hoof, etc.) and one on the skin at the base opening of each ear (see right). They are especially receptive to subtle energy vibrations; for example changes in the weather like a thunderstorm, or even impending, major earth events like an earthquake or hurricane. The Bud chakras located in the feet are often used to source areas of energy in the ground which are beneficial to the animal. When they find these areas they may paw the ground before either laying or rolling on the spot (not to be confused with a dog finding something 'smelly' to roll in!). Standing on such an area can also help ground an animal.

The 21 Minor chakras in animals are sensory centers and can be found, in among other places, on the nose, tail and ears. Whilst the Bud and Minor chakras are smaller energy centers than the Major ones, they are every bit as important and assist in the function of the Major chakras.

174

Below: Illustration showing position of the Major Chakras, the primary Minor Chakra and Bud Chakras on animals. Whilst the illustration is of a horse, the placement is the same for all animals (allowing for scale and body shape). See bottom of page for dog and cat illustrations.

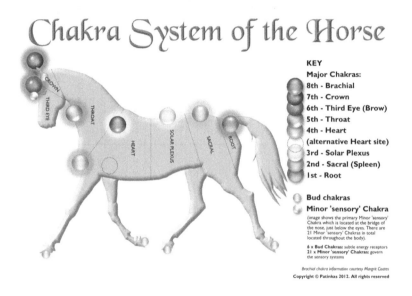

Chakra System of the Horse

KEY

Major Chakras:

8th - Brachial
7th - Crown
6th - Third Eye (Brow)
5th - Throat
4th - Heart
(alternative Heart site)
3rd - Solar Plexus
2nd - Sacral (Spleen)
1st - Root

Bud chakras
Minor 'sensory' Chakra

(image shows the primary Minor 'sensory' Chakra which is located at the bridge of the nose, just below the eyes. There are 21 Minor 'sensory' Chakras in total located throughout the body).

6 x Bud Chakras: subtle energy receptors
21 x Minor 'sensory' Chakras: govern the sensory systems

Brachial chakra information courtesy Margrit Coates

Brief Overview of Animal Chakras:
Location, Function/Purpose, Signs of Imbalance and Body Areas Governed, Gemstones

The 8 Major Chakras

See the following tables:

Chakra	Location	Function Purpose	Signs of imbalance	Body area governed	Gemstones
Brachial (primary 'Major' chakra – healing should start at this chakra)	between shoulders (on a horse, just below where shoulder meets neck)	links all other Major chakras, centre for animal-human bonding, place to start healing	reluctance to be touched (other than for obvious medical reasons: arthritis, inflamed skin, etc), reluctance/refusal to 'connect'	chest, neck, forelimbs, head	Black Tourmaline (if animal is reluctant to connect), Herkimer Diamond, piece of programmed Clear Quartz (click on link for programming info)
Crown	on top of head, between the ears (at the 'poll' on a horse)	connects to spirit	depression, withdrawal	brain, pituitary gland, skin, spine, central and autonomic nervous system, cranio-sacral system	Clear Quartz, Azestulite, Tanzanite, Diamond
Third Eye (Brow)	centre of forehead, just above the eyes	acceptance of self	headaches, bad eyes, distant/distracted	head in general, pineal gland, natural body rhythms, higher mental self	Lapis Lazuli, Fluorite Amethyst, Charoite
Throat	on physical throat (on long-necked animals, over vocal chords)	communication	uncommunicative or excessively noisy, doesn't listen to commands (training	throat, mouth, teeth, jaws (albeit often caused from root-based fear, animals which chew excessively can often benefit from having energy balanced here)	Blue Quartz, Blue Lace Agate, Blue Topaz

Chakra	Location	Function Purpose	Signs of imbalance	Body area governed	Gemstones
Heart	breast/front of chest to behind forelegs (above brisket to breast on a horse)	herd hierarchy (relationships)	sad (recent emotional grief/ separation/loss?), overly possessive, unwilling to interact with other animals, jealous, nervous around other animals for no known reason	heart, lungs, immune system, thymus gland	Rose Quartz, Emerald, Pink Tourmaline, Jade
Solar Plexus	middle of the back	personal power, sense of self (often depleted in domesticated animals)	dejected, withdrawn, aggressive, dominating, no enthusiasm	digestive tract, stomach, liver	Citrine, Tiger Eye, Amber, Topaz
Sacral (Spleen)	lower lumber area, between tail and middle of back (rump or middle of croup on a horse)	sexuality, emotion (emotional loss of animal partner, home, offspring, etc, can often be stored here). Good place to work on when animal in shock whilst waiting for, or en route to vet	over emotional: excessive whining for no obvious reason (exclude medical reasons first), boundary issues: i.e. for a dog/horse: difficulty establishing difference between work (training) time and play (off lead/ lead rope) time	kidneys, adrenal glands, reproductive system, lymphatic system	Carnelian, Coral, Orange Calcite
Root	where tail meets body (hindquarters)	survival, grounding, (this chakra can be especially developed in animals lower down the prey system or food chain, i.e. animals preyed upon by others)	excessively fearful/strong flight reaction, greedy, sluggish, underweight, restless	intestines, gut, hips, hind legs, muscular skeletal system as a whole	Hematite, Garnet, Red Jasper, Unakite

177

Unsurprisingly, most animals' senses or instincts are far more finely tuned and sensitive than humans' (although some animals are more developed than others, like dolphins). As a result, animal chakras are usually far brighter and larger in comparison to ours. Their strong sixth sense emanates from the primary sensory center; one of the 21 Minor chakras. This is located at the bridge of the nose, below the Third Eye or Brow chakra. Animals are constantly absorbing and computing sensory information, far more so than humans, owing to their reliance on instinct for survival. Aside from using the Bud chakras in their feet as mentioned above, they may also be seen rubbing a part of their body against a tree, rolling on the ground or even rubbing up against their fellow animal or human companions to stimulate a chakra. An animal that has suffered from physical, mental or emotional trauma, however, may not always be able to repair the resulting energetic imbalance and this is where we find signs of disease (dis-ease) present.

Each chakra corresponds to an aspect of the self: thought, emotion, senses, instinct and so on. Whilst governing the same physical areas, animal chakras have, however, developed or evolved slightly differently from those of humans. This can be further defined with differences between domestic and wild animals. For example, you tend to find a more developed Heart chakra in wild animals (strong herd hierarchy) plus a more pronounced Root chakra (stronger sense of survival). With a wild horse, you will see a stronger flight response (Solar plexus chakra) than in a Thoroughbred, which is a man-made breed. Then we have neutering or castration of domestic animals which strongly affects the Sacral (or Spleen) chakra.

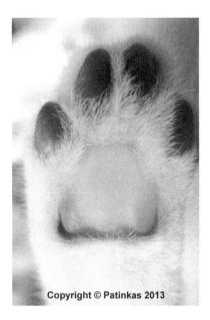

Above: Photo showing position of Bud Chakra on a cat's paw.

21 Minor Chakras

Location: throughout the body.

Function: govern the sensory systems. The most important Minor chakra is located at the bridge of the nose, below the eyes (under the Brow or Third Eye chakra – see diagrams).

Bud Chakras

Location: one on the base of each foot (two in birds) and one at the base of each ear - under the flap, just at the opening

Function: senses, subtle energy receptors

Below: Illustration showing positions of Major Chakras, primary Minor (sensory) Chakra and Bud Chakras on a dog and a cat

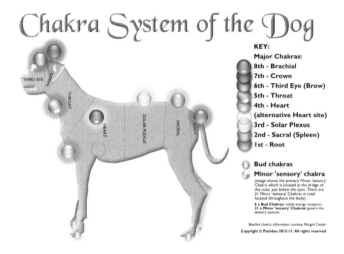

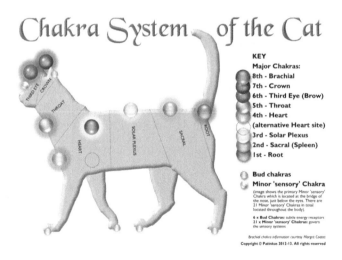

Dog's Minor 'sensory' chakras in action

Same picture but with chakra shown! (Major, Minor & Bud)

Use of this Article

You are more than welcome to use this article for your own purposes, or for reproduction (on paper or on the web), including illustrations (we are not precious about our work - it feels good to share!)—we merely ask that if it is going to be reproduced, that you attribute full copyright to Patinkas as shown below:

For the pictures/illustrations, copyright to read (in a prominent position): Copyright image provided courtesy of Patinkas © 2009.

For the copy/text, copyright to read (in a prominent position): Copyright article provided courtesy of Patinkas © 2009.

If you want images without the copyright text showing (so you can enter our copyright information separately), please e-mail us and we will send you images in JPG or GIF format (please specify).

With all bright blessing from the Patinkas Team.

<www.patinkas.co.uk/Chakra_System_of_Animals/chakra_system_of_animals.html>

Appendix B: Finding a Reiki Master - Questions to Ask

Before you select the Reiki Master with whom you wish to learn, you might consider asking the following questions. I have included my answers to these questions, some of which might be repeated from the book.

Do you teach the traditional Usui method?

I teach the traditional Usui method as learned from the Master who taught me. This is the four-level Reiki as taught by Dr. Arthur Robertson.

I have not added to this traditional teaching, other than to give an overview of the energy field and chakras and grounding.

If you do a search on the Internet, you will find many variations of Reiki, such as Reiki Plus. I suggest that you ask the person who you contact what has been added, where this originates, and why he or she has chosen to make additions to the traditional method.

What is the maximum number of students you accept in a class?

When I began teaching, I accepted a maximum of eight students in any level class. With time and experience, I have learned that I can comfortably teach and hold a group of 12 students without taking away from the intimacy of the group or lengthening the time of the course beyond 11-12 hours.

Learning in a group setting is a rich experience. The student gets to meet like-minded persons with which he or she can share and learn from during the course, as each sharing from another student adds to what may be taught.

The collective energy of the group creates a strong energy field, which enhances the Reiki energy in the room. This in turn enhances the absorption of the Reiki energies during the attunements and the treatment exchanges.

What is your lineage of Reiki Masters?

You may be curious to know the origin of these sacred teachings that the person will transmit to you. My lineage can be found in Appendix C.

Can you describe your apprenticeship and the length of time you took to become a Reiki Master?

I took my level 1 and 2 in 1994, my level 3 in 1996, and my master level in 1997, all with the same Reiki Master. Once I completed the Reiki Master course, I had several meetings with my Reiki Master to answer questions and review progress. Unfortunately, he then moved away to Portugal, and I lost touch with him for quite some time.

In order to complement my Master training, I then did the Master training again with a second Reiki Master.

How long have you been teaching and how regularly do you teach?

I started teaching in 1998 and have been teaching several times a year since, more so since I opened my office and practice in 2002. I presently teach Levels 1 and 2 four times per year, Level 3 two or three times per year, and the master level when I have students. I have currently trained about 12 Reiki Masters.

Will I get a chance to practice during the course?

During all the levels I teach, my students get to practice all the techniques, whether they be self-treatment, giving and receiving a treatment or technique with another person or a group, or attunements.

This is important, as I am able to observe, assist, and guide as required. Many questions come up for the students after the treatments and the answers, explanations, or ensuing discussions are a rich source of learning.

I have had some novice students get dizzy or faint from giving a treatment for the first time or get very hot from channeling the energy. Without practice time during the course, the Reiki Master cannot answer concerns and be with the student or the client at these moments, which can be an unpleasant experience for the giver and the receiver.

What are the different levels in the method that you teach?

In the method that I teach, there are four levels:

- Reiki 1: treating yourself and others.

- Reiki 2: Symbols are taught that increase the healing power and allow distance healing. A variation of the method called emotional/mental Reiki is also taught.

- Reiki 3: Introduction of the first Master symbol and two new techniques provided.

- Reiki Master/Teacher: Master and Teaching level.

At each of the levels, I review the Reiki principles and anything that might be unclear from the other levels, as well as give time for the students to share their experience of the previous course, treatments given, and their current practice.

How many hours of teaching are involved in each level?

The duration of my courses usually go beyond the minimum required by the Canadian Reiki Association, with which I am registered as a Teacher.

<u>Reiki 1</u>

The Canadian Reiki Association requires a minimum of eight hours for level 1. I teach this level in ten to twelve hours, usually in an evening and a day. I believe that this time is necessary for a first-time exposure to energy and a better integration of what is learnt. The night offers integration time.

<u>Reiki 2</u>

The Canadian Reiki Association requires a minimum of eight hours for level 2. I also teach this level in an eight-hour day.

<u>Reiki 3</u>

The Canadian Reiki Association requires a minimum of eight hours for level 3. I teach this level in a minimum of eight hours, including the main teaching, assigned homework, and a final individual meeting with each student.

The homework, which is in the form of questions to reflect on plus reports on two of several in-person and distance treatments, ensures that the student actually performs treatments and allows a deepening of all that has been learned to date and inspires the student to take the time to study and report on the experience of giving and receiving treatments.

Once I receive the assignments, I review them, provide comments, and return them to the students. I only issue the certificate at the final individual meeting with the student during which any questions are addressed and at which the student is invited to share the individual experience and journey of self-healing.

Not all Reiki Masters provide this follow-up and guidance. I have found that at this level, this is invaluable for the student/practitioner who by now is usually interested in practicing Reiki more often with others or even professionally.

Master level

The teaching at the Master/Teacher level starts with a powerful attunement ritual and a new symbol. Later, when the student is ready, he or she learns to teach and attune students at all levels.

Some Reiki Masters offer the training over a period of time supported by homework assignments and regular meetings. Others offer the training without this support, but hopefully remain available to answer questions and give guidance when needed.

Personally, I require that a person study with me over a period of eight months to one year, starting with the initiation ritual and continuing with attending my classes as observers; practicing the art; and doing the assigned readings, assignments, and associated reports on six of the thirty treatments that I require they do over that time period.

The Master students work at their own pace and benefit from ongoing contact with me, supported by review and comments on the work submitted. This ensures that the students integrate the teachings and can attend classes free of having to teach or learn the material. They are then available to take in what I say and how I teach without pressure.

In addition, I coach them on starting their own practice and how to develop a clientele. They are required to attend and then perhaps lead a Reiki Share, which is a get-together of Reiki practitioners and newcomers to Reiki to share experiences, meditate, answer questions, and exchange treatments.

The training is complete when I am satisfied that they have met all the requirements; have integrated the heart and soul of the method; and will be able to receive, accompany, support, and guide potential students through the different levels from novice to Master/Teacher. I can then rest assured that they will faithfully transmit the learning to their own students with dedication, heart, and experience.

The above is tailored as required for individual needs.

Is it wise or possible to change Reiki Masters from one level to the other?

Reiki 1: This level includes four initiation rituals.

Reiki 2: This level includes two initiation rituals, with three symbols.

Reiki 3: This level includes one initiation ritual, with one symbol.

Master level: This level includes two initiation rituals, with one symbol.

Do you issue certificates for each level?

I issue certificates for each level, signed as a registered teacher with the Canadian Reiki Association.

Is it wise or possible to change Reiki Masters from one level to the other?

I allow my students to study with a different Master and return with me at any time during their training. This offers the student the chance to see a different perspective of how each Master has integrated the method, teaches it, and lives it.

What is especially important is that the student takes the course from an active Reiki Master with whom he or she feels comfortable and who is a good model of living the teachings and the principles.

If you change Reiki Masters, be sure to get a certificate for each level that you have taken as it is highly probable that the new Master will ask you for these before he or she accepts to teach you at a higher level.

Do you offer any support and follow-up for your students?

It is important that the Master be available to answer questions that might come up while you are integrating Reiki, especially for the three or four weeks following the course.

After levels 1 and 2, I remain available for periodic questions from students as they integrate the teachings and the Reiki energy. As described above, level 3 and the master level allow a lot of time for support during the training.

I currently make my office available for Reiki Shares that are led by Reiki Masters I have trained and attend when I am available.

Are you a member of a Reiki association?

I am registered as a Reiki Master/Teacher with the Canadian Reiki Association (www.reiki.ca).

Appendix C: Lineage of Reiki Master Roland Bérard

MIKAO USUI

DR. CHURIJO HAYASHI

HAWAYO TAKATA

IRIS ISHIKURO

DR. ARTHUR ROBERTSON

ROGER FOISY

BERNARD GRENIER (CHETAN ASEEM)

ROLAND BÉRARD

Appendix D: Reiki Resources

This appendix presents some of my favorite books and some of my favorite music.

Books

Reiki

Horan P. (1990). *Empowerment through Reiki: The path to personal and global transformation.* Twin Lakes, WI: Lotus Light Publications.

This is still one of my favorite books on Reiki. Paula Horan does an excellent job of presenting this wonderful healing art that has its origins in Tibet.

Lübeck, W. (1996). *Way of the heart,* Twin Lakes, WI: Lotus Press.

I love the way Walter shows us how Reiki is linked to the heart and how he suggests working with our relationship to the Inner Child.

Honervogt, T. (1998). *The power of Reiki: An ancient hands-on healing technique.* New York, NY: Owl Books-Henry Holt and Company.

A beautifully illustrated book on Reiki that presents the essentials and how, and on what, to use Reiki. The illustrations are exquisite. Just looking at a few pages will incite you to pick it up and bring it home.

Lübeck, W., Petter, F. A. & Rand, W. L. (2001). *The spirit of Reiki.* Twin Lakes, WI: Lotus Press.

These three Reiki Masters dug deeper into the history of Reiki and present lots of interesting information about how Reiki is still very active in Japan, as well as some original documents from Usui and Dr. Hayashi. It shows that the traditional story of Reiki and its legacy are somewhat different than what was reported and handed down by Hawayo Takata.

Haberly, H. J. O. (1990). *Hawayo Takata's story.* Olney, MD: Archedigm Publications.

A wonderful and lively account of this great Reiki Master's life and her passion for bringing Reiki to the world. We owe her a lot for her devotion, passion and gutsiness. The words I remember from the book are those that Mrs. Takata was always saying: "Do Reiki, do Reiki, do Reiki."

Energy Field

Brennan, B. (1988). *Hands of light.* New York, NY: Bantam Books.

This book is a classic on the energy field and energy healing. Barbara presents the complete energy field, chakras, characterology (defense strategies), and more. Answers are included to many questions you may have been wondering about.

Brennan, B. (1993). *Light emerging.* New York, NY: Bantam Books.

In this book, Barbara presents the energy field and the path to healing in a way that is easy to grasp and understand. She introduces the dimensions of the Hara and Core Star.

Judith, A. (2004). *Eastern body, Western mind.* Berkeley, CA: Celestial Arts.

This book is a treasure. Judith describes all aspects of the chakras and explains the physical, emotional, mental, psychological and spiritual aspects of the chakras. She details how life experience affects the chakras and what it means when a chakra is functional or dysfunctional, overused (excessive) or underused (deficient). She gives practical and meaningful ways to heal each chakra. This book is a must for anyone working with chakras or wanting to understand them.

Dale, C. (2009). *The subtle body: An encyclopedia of your energetic anatomy.* Boulder, CO: Sounds True.

Cindi does a really great job of describing the energy field and many different approaches to healing. This is a great resource book.

Music

Reiki Whale Song, Kamal

Beautifully interwoven with whale songs, this provides a relaxing and nourishing atmosphere for healings and massage.

Transformation - Music for Massage, Michael Benghiat

Very relaxing music for massage.

Crystal Silence I - The Silence Within, Robert Haig Coxon

The soft repetition on this CD is meditative, and I love using it during healings.

By Celtic Waters, Ashmore/Willow Sanctuary

Another CD I love to use with beautiful nature sounds.

Essence, Deva Premal

This is Deva's classic CD on which she chants sacred Sanskrit mantra. I really love this CD, as it sets a great mood for healings.

Embrace, Deva Premal

Another CD by Deva that has wonderful tracks of chants and mantras.

Healing Music of the Goddess Volumes 1 and 2, Marjorie Valeri

Marjorie channeled divine harp music during Heyon channelings by Barbara Brennan. Angelic harp that is wonderful for healing sessions. It is available through her on-line store at

www.barbarabrennan.com

Reiki Hands of Light, Deuter

This CD has excellent and light music to elevate the spirit. I use this one a lot during healings and initiations.

Reiki Offering, Shastro and Nadama

Another CD that is light and wonderful for healings.

Appendix E: Reiki Research

There is a lot of research being done on Reiki to support its effectiveness and increase its credibility. Reiki is already being widely applied in hospitals and health centers.

Here are a few websites that support and/or present research on Reiki.

Center for Reiki Research - www.centerforreikiresearch.org

The Center for Reiki Research, including Reiki in Hospitals, was founded by William Rand. You can join the website for free and obtain access to the extensive information that can be found on the site.

Reiki, Medicine and Self Care, **Pamela Miles** - www.reikiinmedicine.org/medical-papers

Numerous articles supporting Reiki can be found on this website.

Reiki Council - www.reikicouncil.org.uk

Many studies are cited on the Research page.

Reiki Australia - www.reikiaustralia.com.au

This website presents Reiki research from 1995 to 2011.

Appendix F: Testimonials on the Use of Reiki and the Journey

Included in this appendix are testimonials of the journey through Reiki related by some of my students.

Jean Beaulieu

For the last few years, I have been on an extremely nourishing path of personal growth. Approximately one year before my first Reiki initiation, I experienced many intensive events that led me to many discoveries about myself. Following this, I had a strong intuition to create something new in my life, and so I decided to experience Reiki. I asked to be guided to find a Reiki Master whose energy and ethics would suit me. That is when I found Roland's website and began my journey.

During the first evening of the level 1 course, I was filled with such a pleasant and powerful energy that I felt at one with Creation. I remember that after the course, I stopped to eat at a very busy restaurant in which the energy was very chaotic. I beamed Reiki and instantly the place became calm and harmonious. I felt that people could themselves feel the difference in their state of being.

When I got home, my partner was experiencing a headache and back pain. I placed my hand on her back and felt a wave of energy flow through me and then move through her. She was very surprised at how powerful this energy was, and she was completely relieved of her headache and back pain. I fell asleep that night while giving myself a Reiki treatment and I had a profound and restful sleep. Upon waking, I was completely inhabited by Reiki and a strong sense of well-being.

I would send Reiki everywhere around me. During the first level initiation, I deeply felt the sacredness of this approach, the high frequency vibration of the Universal Energy and the life force that was so pleasant to experience. That weekend was very revealing and was, to my surprise, only the beginning. Let me explain.

Every day I would give myself a treatment and I would feel a huge benefit. I would apply Reiki to almost everything and I could clearly see its impact on situations, matter, and people. At night, as I put my baby to bed, I would give him a Reiki treatment and I noticed that he would fall asleep faster and be filled with a sense of well-being. As a matter of fact, I have been giving him a treatment every night for two years now. After seeing me practice Reiki so much, my oldest (six-year-old) daughter is now giving herself a treatment every night and loves to offer her services when someone is not feeling well. She is very good and very efficient.

The week following my first level, I bought three books on Reiki and immediately joined the Canadian Reiki Association. My goal was to complete my twenty-four case studies in three months. To my great surprise, I actually did 54 treatments in those three months. The more I practiced Reiki, the more it spoke to me and guided me as to what I needed to transform in myself and on the meaning of my life. I felt Reiki purify me as much, if not more, than those I was treating. My clients were experiencing many benefits and seeing results. In my first year, I treated close to 250 persons. Of these, about 90% experienced direct benefits and the other 10% seemed to feel at least a great sense of well-being.

As I tracked the experience of the 10% from a distance, I could see their lives shifting, and I witnessed them having experiences that brought them further along on their path. I even had people that did not believe in Reiki at all come for treatments, only to have their lives completely transformed. They subsequently became open to this dimension.

So I can really ascertain that this was only the beginning. Notwithstanding all the beautiful healing and transformation I witnessed in my clients, I was mostly surprised and touched by the presence of Reiki within me; a presence that spoke to me, inspired me, motivated me and sometimes "pushed" me. I feel how it resonated with me and I sometimes see its energy gently swirling around me.

My Reiki adventure progressed very quickly and continually brought me all kinds of self-discoveries. Each time I took another level I felt really ready and I could tell that my soul was waiting for this event. I would never have believed that I would experience such deep contact with the symbols in level 2. Each one of the levels has inspired me and activated a new light within me. Since my initiation to the symbols, they feel more like energy of support and accompaniment rather than a "technique" that I apply. Each time, they are like energies or beings acting on their own. I feel there is still a lot to discover about my relationship to the symbols and that they will yield many gifts.

I am very happy with my journey. This new breath of life will help me realize my mission, my life's work. Today, I feel more myself, more present, more in my body, and more inspired. I feel that Reiki is continually tuning my being and that I am now solidly on the path of transformation. I can see this path in my everyday life. I have more trust in my energetic capability, I am more open to healing, and I feel that every moment is enlightening, harmonizing, and healing.

Thank you, Roland, for your support, your own evolution and your intention. I am convinced that my Reiki experience would not have been the same if it had not been supported by your vibration and your love, your ethical sense of energy, your approach of keeping it simple and working with the frequencies, your mastery of grounding and the Hara alignment, your loving presence, your sense of the sacred, your love for Reiki and energy, your continual attention to keep us present. All this, I am sure, has allowed me to have the most divine of experiences. It has allowed me an intimate and privileged experience of the Reiki energy. The Reiki Master that you are inspires and guides me. You are an excellent model of a healing facilitator and wisdom that I wish to multiply by initiating others myself.

Thank you, thank you, thank you!

Dimitra Panaritis

Reiki benefits my body, mind, soul, and environment.

Reiki transforms me each time. After each session, my external world may remain the same but my vision becomes different. I am happy and in a state of bliss simply because I am.

Reiki teaches me to let go of attachments, expectations and answers.

Reiki allows me to experience the perfection of Oneness in the Universe.

Reiki instills peace, love, joy, passion, safety within and the faith that all is perfect as is.

Reiki heals and allows my True Self to reveal itself.

Roland, thank you so much for your guidance, kindness, and generosity that gave me the courage to take my practice to another level.

Forever Grateful,
With love,

Dimitra Panaritis

Barbara Plascencia

Level 1

Reiki Usui Level 1 was a very intense experience for me. When I first heard about Reiki it was through someone who was using it to heal from cancer. I had been in and out of the hospital a couple of times during a whole year between 2002 and 2003. The doctors could not figure out what my problem was. At first they thought it was my appendix and so they removed it, but the pain came back. After getting different opinions, a doctor finally told me it was stress. I thought to myself that it was almost impossible for me to be stressed. I loved everything about my life and I didn't consider myself as stressed. Dr. A. M. suggested I take pills to control my pain, but I couldn't feel any improvement when I did.

For some reason this mysterious technique called Reiki kept coming to my mind and, following my impulse, I decided to take a course. I was 19. When I got to the first class I realized there were many people from different walks of life and with different intentions to take the course; not everyone was sick like me. Some people were trying to add it as a tool for the massage techniques, others were dealing with the loss of their loved ones and some others were in some sort of spiritual journey. I was impressed by how many people were gathered in the same room to learn something I knew very little about.

I couldn't stop crying during the first attunement. I began to think about my life and my relationship with my father. I realized it was time to forgive him for whatever it was that hurt me. I resented him for not being there enough, yet I was never really willing to be around him for some reason. I could not understand why these thoughts would come to my mind. I was there to heal a pain I had in my stomach.

205

When the time came for us to practice a treatment, I began to see images of a hospital and a person saying goodbye, the woman to whom I was giving a treatment was actually trying to overcome the death of her husband and whatever I described to her made sense to her. When she gave me a treatment in exchange, the Reiki teacher passed by my table and put his hands on my stomach, my pain disappeared almost instantly.

I couldn't understand why this was happening. I sometimes even tell myself that this story makes no sense whatsoever, but that was how it happened. After that class I kept on using Reiki to work on myself and with time I learnt that spontaneous healing could not happen at will and that Reiki was mostly a complement to traditional medicine.

Level 2

Reiki Usui Level 2 came to me in a very special time of my life. I had been living in Canada for a couple of months and I had decided to continue my learning. I remember that my cousin had just been diagnosed with some form of cancer and he was only 17. During the class, I asked if we could do a distance healing for him. Because I lived far away, I knew little about his life or what other treatments he was undergoing, but I do remember that my family back in Mexico was having trouble finding a solution. After the distance treatment a solution was found and the cancer is no longer there; today my cousin is alive and well. Was it Reiki? Was it not? I will never know. All I know is that after the treatment something opened up to find a solution.

Level 3

When I got to Reiki Usui Level 3, I was facing many of the choices I had made when I was nineteen. Reiki level 3 was a level of personal growth and opening. I began to share Reiki much more and to feel much more comfortable about my path. I had no idea I would continue to level 4, but a year later I did.

Master Level

The master level was a very challenging level for me. I had to begin sharing my story and journey with others in a more serious way. I learned what the electromagnetic field was and the impact you can have on people. I noticed that being a Reiki Master was not something you could take lightly since you have a responsibility to transmit a very important technique to those who are called to learn it. I thought I was taking the master level just to honor the tradition that had healed me, but it turned out that I had reached that level because I was unknowingly ready to share the Universal Energy of Love that is Reiki. I wish I could explain what happened to me during this level, but to be honest there are no words. Reiki is a surprising technique that definitely works in all levels of your life and no matter how much you try to understand it, your experience is the only thing that can really explain what it really is.

General

Integrating Reiki in my life has opened me to explore realms that I never thought I would be in touch with. I have had the opportunity to meet incredible people and make many of my dreams come true. I know that a lot of people realize their dreams without using Reiki, but in my case most of my deepest desires were attained through the use of Reiki.

I have used Reiki to recover lost items, ask for health, and sometimes even to ask for good grades or the wisdom to attain them. Reiki has been an amazing tool that works, whether or not you believe in it.

Karine Lapointe

We often ask ourselves the question "What is the true meaning of life, why do we exist?" We try to understand the sense of injustice, of dis-ease and disease... My mother was sick during my whole childhood and is still suffering from fibromyalgia. Why was she suffering while others were not?

Reiki came to me as a revelation while I was pondering these questions and thinking about my desire to help those I love. With this short initiation, I could help relieve my mother's suffering. I could, in this way, return all the love she has given me. It could be my way of saying thank you. So, I took the course with the aim of helping others. I also wanted to find my true life path, my role on this Earth.

Everything was about to change. I never suspected that Reiki would be the most precious gift I could offer myself. By wanting to create well-being in others, I did not know that I would be the first to benefit from it. When life is but a fog permeated with doubt, we are on a quest to make sense of it. What is my path? I did not realize that I was wandering away from it and not moving ahead by wanting to do it all at the same time.

Reiki is the lighthouse that lights up the path from afar. In the beginning, there are initiations and the 21-day period of purification. I gave myself Reiki every day; I felt more and more relaxed. I gained more clarity on my existential questions. Emotional blocks and repressed pain from difficult life experiences were cleared. I cried a lot, even though I never cried before. I understood that this period of purification was a huge cleansing of my being. In life, we have a tendency to take care of the physical, but we forget our mental, our soul. I now feel that all my blocks were expressed in my bouts of crying. It was difficult to understand while it was happening, but I felt great afterwards.

I now feel lighter. I am open and happy. I understand my body better and I now know that I must listen to it when it sends me messages. I understand my inner voice better and I have more confidence in my intuition.

Reiki allows us to connect to our inner self. For a long time, I refused to hear the messages from my intuition and my body and I strayed. Now, I listen and reclaim my confidence and my abilities. I also help those around me to find their way and return to well-being through my treatments.

Since my initiations to Reiki, I am connected to my body and my spirituality. This has guided me to meditate and give meaning to my life. I have had many extraordinary encounters with others. A series of events have helped me to go forward. I meet people that bring answers to my questions and I have realized that this is not by chance. We are all connected and I have learned to make concrete requests to life. Everything that I ask for manifests itself. This allows me to believe in my ability to change things and to become a better person.

It is now my turn to bring well-being to others. I want to thank Roland Bérard for initiating me into Reiki and all those that work to bring light to the world's darkness to awaken the planet. It has changed my life and now everything makes sense.

Taline Bedakelian

Prior to taking my first Reiki course, I was a person who was constantly dissatisfied and unhappy. I felt as though I was always searching—searching for what I did not know. I felt as though I had a mission but I did not know what it was, and I felt a pressure because I felt as though time was passing and I was still not doing what I was supposed to do.

I have always had the ability to intuitively know what people were feeling and what they were going through but I did not know how to integrate this ability into my life. If anything, I shut it off because it did not serve me much. I had a lot of internal pain that I did not know what to do with. I was not even aware of the origins of my misery and pain.

Reiki 1 was a God-sent [sic] to me. When I was initiated, I felt right there and then as though I had finally found what it was that I had been searching for, for so long. I felt as though all the misery and pain were suddenly uplifted from my shoulders and that I could actually start seeing life and my experiences through a clearer lens. I felt as though I was not alone and that I was held in the warmest, most loving arms. I felt a support and a love coming to me from beyond. Reiki 1 definitely left me in a place of peace, love, joy, and harmony.

Reiki 2 was a little more challenging. Reiki 2 started up a discontent and a frustration in my soul. It started my journey of looking inward and discovering who I was and what my issues were. It caused chaos that forced me to make changes with certain situations in my life which no longer served my growth. It started me on my journey of questioning beliefs that I have carried with me throughout my life.

Reiki 3 brought more peace into my life whilst continuing my inner cleansing. I am now a much more self-aware individual. I am beginning to see what my issues are and why and where they come from. The internal cleansing and chaos had gained speed and I am now going through it much more quickly. I am learning to hold onto my peace regardless of what is going on. I am learning to love myself and have more compassion for myself. I am remembering old childhood memories that have been blocked out throughout decades. It is a very challenging period and yet my evolution has made tremendous leaps within the last year and a half.

This is not to say that it has been easy. On the contrary, it has made me seek out and find help in order to sort through and clear a lot of my internal pain. I have also realized that I need to clear myself in order to make room for more love, more compassion, and more energy. Each time I clear and make more room for energy, my ability to help others increases and I am able to channel a higher vibration.

Appendix G: Effective Therapies and Tools for Transformation

In the first part of this appendix, I present the approaches that I have personally studied and experienced and believe are effective in self-development and personal transformation on the healing journey.

Following this, I briefly outline some of the other approaches that I have been drawn to experience, read extensively on and have partially studied.

All these have influenced how I work with clients.

Essentially all the therapies presented are taught through experiential learning, in that you integrate the material by working through your own process as you learn it.

I have studied and integrated the following in my practice:

- Reiki – Master degree in 1997.

- Brennan Healing Science – Diploma of the four-year program in 2002 and the two-year advanced studies in Teacher Training in 2005.

- Hakomi – Therapist since 2005 and Trainer since 2009.

- Emotional Freedom Technique – I hold the original basic (2003) and advanced (2004) certificates issued by Gary Craig in the early days, that have now been replaced with Certificate Training, which I have not pursued.

- ThetaHealing – basic and advanced course in 2002.

- Somatic-Psychoeducation and fasciatherapy (Danis Bois).

As I write this book, I have completed the second year of the four-year program in Core Energetics. I have done a lot of personal work using this modality at the Barbara Brennan School of Healing and in my own personal therapy.

The approaches described herein will surely be of interest to any practitioner wishing to deepen their personal process and professional training.

What is Effective Therapy?

Everyone has a different doorway to healing. There is not one magical therapy that works for everybody and a different doorway may be more appropriate at one time than another.

A lot has changed since Freud's work that introduced therapy to our modern world. Analytic/talk therapy has evolved into approaches that now include the body/mind connection.

My personal experience has been that the therapies that include the body/mind connection combined with energy and consciousness tend to be more rapid, effective, and long-lasting because they by-pass the rational mind and get to the places where emotions are stored and trapped in the body, and the body does not lie.

I can explain to you all day what a juicy strawberry tastes like, but if you have never tasted one, I will not be able to convey to you how it really tastes. The only way for you to know is to experience it yourself. It is the same with images and beliefs that cause suffering. I cannot convince you that you do not have to do it alone and that help is available around you if you have the belief that no one is there for you or ever will be. The only way you can transform that belief is to actually have the experience of letting someone help.

Once you have experienced something, you cannot deny your experience. This presents new possibilities for being and when these experiences are repeated, change can take place and remain.

Body-centered therapies use the body/mind connection to access core material. Gestures, posture, body-language, muscular tensions and development patterns, tone of voice, and rolling the eyes are but a few of the ways the body can be an indicator of the images and beliefs you hold about the world.

Energy work will open up stuck places in the energy field and lead to more harmonious experiences. Body-centered work will release blocks and trapped emotions so that they can be felt and worked with in a healing way. Bringing consciousness to what we have not been able to see is the first, and the key, step in the healing journey of transforming experience to make life more nourishing and pleasurable.

The combination of energy, body-centered work, and conscious awakening are powerful and rapid transformational tools when they are used in collaboration by a competent therapist and a client who is curious and willing to explore deeply-held emotions, beliefs, and images. The work requires a clear intention, courage, determination, and time, but it does yield results.

And yet there are times when talking is necessary to help make sense of what has come up. It is easier to let go of the anger or resistance attached to an experience if one can make sense of the experience; only then can forgiveness happen. This paves the way for a transformation of beliefs and images. The doorway to making sense and reframing the experience is often through the rational mind. Therefore, talking, reasoning, and rationalizing have their useful place in holistic therapy, as long as they are not the principle or the only options offered.

I hope you will take the time to explore some of these approaches for your own personal development to access your joy and passion in a way you never thought possible as you continue on your own journey.

Therapies and tools I have studied and/or currently practice

Brennan Healing Science

The Method

Brennan Healing Science is taught in a four-year course at the Barbara Brennan School of Healing. It is an intensive program that teaches how one can facilitate healing by working deeply in the four dimensions of the Human Energy Field—the physical, the aura (chakras and energy bodies), the Hara (level of intention), and the Core Star (level of pure essence).

The basic curriculum at the school includes approximately sixty techniques to work in these four dimensions as well as High Sense Perception (HSP, perceiving the energy field), cellular awareness, personal development through psych-spiritual conscious awakening skills, and professional practice. Also included are courses on how one can bridge this work with the traditional medical professions and the community of complementary and alternative medicine (CAM).

The curriculum is enriched with yearly art projects, ceremony, a graduating year practical project, and the presentation of a case study.

The student's growth is supported throughout the four years with individual and group therapy, as well as continuous follow-up and mentoring from the teaching staff. The graduating Brennan Healing Science Practitioner is thus able to maintain deep contact with the self and other in facilitating the healing process of the client.

The program is recognized as a Bachelor in Energetic Healing Science by the State of Florida and the school is currently working to gain accreditation in all US states.

Barbara opened her school in 1982 and currently runs a school in the USA.

Barbara has a solid scientific background as a physicist working for NASA, and she has done extensive personal development work. She is a Core Energetics Therapist and Pathwork Helper and holds a Doctorate in both Physics and Theology.

Since I am often asked the question about the comparison between Reiki and Brennan Healing Science, I have written an article that is available on my website that presents the similarities and differences in the two approaches. It can be accessed here:

<www.rolandberard.com/Production/EN/MyArticles.htm>

How I integrate this method into my approach

Energy work (a combination of Reiki and Brennan Healing Science) is foundational in my practice.

Every time I see a client, I do a reading of the energy field and track the progress from one session to the next.

Unless specifically requested by the client not to do energy work, I will usually include energy balancing in the first session to open the field and start the flow of energy where it has previously been blocked.

In subsequent sessions, I use energy work as required, but there is always an energetic transmission because of the way I have learned to prepare and hold my own energy field when I meet clients. The client's energy field will adjust itself by induction to mine where my field is more harmonious.

Tracking the energy field with the Chakra Charting Method© that I have developed is a visual way to follow the progress and see where the field is opening and where it still needs support.

Books

Brennan, B. (1998). *Hands of light*. New York, NY: Bantam Books.

Barbara Brennan's classic first book presents the aura or energy field, which is comprised of energy bodies and chakras. She describes the many aspects of how disease originates in the auric field before manifesting on the physical reality and how this can be healed by working through the energy field.

Brennan, B. (1993). *Light emerging*. New York, NY: Bantam Books.

In her second book, Barbara introduces the Hara and Core Star dimensions, the various aspects and phases of the healing journey and the interactions of, and in, the human energy field in relationship.

Brennan, B. (1999). *Seeds of the spirit*. Barbara Brennan Inc.

This is a series that contains the channeling of Barbara's guide Heyoan during the school year. There is a book for each school year, during which the current topics are addressed by Heyoan.

These channelings have been edited into prose form to make them easier to read.

Websites

BBSH, Barbara Brennan School of Healing

Hakomi

The Method

Donna Martin, Hakomi trainer, writes "Hakomi is an experiential method of assisted self-discovery that uses "little experiments in mindfulness" to discover how one's experience is organized by habits and unconscious attitudes and beliefs.

As such, Hakomi is a true InSight method, one which is "therapeutic" when used to support one's own or another's healing of emotional and psychological issues. Hakomi is also effective in many non-therapy situations involving human relations, from teaching to parenting and from customer service to hospice work. "

In Hakomi, we:

- Use mindfulness to create an inner space where one can observe whatever is present.

- Have an experimental attitude.

- Focus on present-moment experience. We are more interested in the storyteller than the story and we do not focus on the past or the future, but on what is happening in the moment.

- Move towards nourishment by creating nourishing experiences to transform limiting beliefs, habits, and images that may have led to the missing experience of allowing nourishment in.

Hakomi is based on five principles:

- Mindfulness: the non-judgmental observer of what is present in the moment.

- Mind-body holism: the fact that whatever is in the body is related to whatever is happening in the mind and vice versa.

- Non-violence: the focus is never forcing to break through blocks, fears, and resistance, but rather on supporting them so they can be seen or heard, acknowledged, understood and dissolved in a loving and safe container of self-discovery.

- Organicity: the fact that healing is a spontaneous process that is organic in nature, and the fact that all the resources are within the client and will emerge when we create conditions where the unconscious will be invited to and feel safe enough to reveal itself, cooperate, and actually lead the healing process.

- Unicity: in that we are all related and everything we do affects others around us.

The Hakomi therapist's role is to listen and follow rather than talk and direct by closely tracking and contacting the present moment experience in a state of loving presence, a key skill taught in Hakomi.

With the above conditions in place, Hakomi is a very direct and rapid route to the unconscious and it is a very effective therapy for personal development.

Hakomi was created by the late Ron Kurtz, who was influenced by BioEnergetics, Feldenkrais, Gestalt, Buddhism, and the Tao Te Ching, among others. The use of mindfulness and the technique of taking over are two of the innovative approaches to therapy created by Ron.

The basics of the Hakomi Method is learned in various formats of the two-year program, after which a student becomes a Certified Hakomi Therapist upon demonstrating competency to two trainers.

The Hakomi Method has been widely taught by the Hakomi Institute in many countries since the 1970s.

The Refined Method of Assisted Self-Discovery was later developed by Ron Kurtz. The Refined Method is taught by the Hakomi Educational Network (HEN) of teachers and trainers.

How I integrate this method into my approach

Hakomi is totally integrated into my approach. I try to do everything in a "Hakomi way," and I use it in part or all of a session with my clients. Hakomi has taught me to trust the organicity and spontaneity of the healing process and to follow the client rather than lead and direct a session. It has taught me to track the present moment experience and contact it so that the client can see and feel that I am really present and following. It has taught me to move towards nourishment and to support defenses rather than try to break through them.

Most importantly, for me, Hakomi has helped me to go from "DOING" healing work to "BEING" with the client. What needs to happen then emerges effortlessly much of the time and the healing happens more quickly and organically.

That is why I now refer to myself as a healing facilitator rather then an energy worker or therapist.

Books

Kurtz, R. S. (1990). *Body-centered psychotherapy: The Hakomi Method.* Mondocino, CA: LifeRhythm.

This is Ron's original book on the method and contains all the elements of his early form of Hakomi, many of which are still very relevant.

Johanson, G., & Kurtz, R. S. (1991). *Grace unfolding: Psychotherapy in the spirit of the Tao-te Ching.* New York, NY: Bell Tower.

This wonderful book brilliantly demonstrates how Hakomi is the Tao Te Ching of psychotherapy.

Fisher, R. (2002*). Experiential psychotherapy with couples: A guide for the creative pragmatist.* Phoenix, AZ: Zeig, Tucker and Theisen Inc.

This book does a tremendous job of showing us how the Hakomi method can be used for couples work and how loving presence, mindfulness, an experimental attitude, and moving towards nourishment in a non-violent way will work deeply and quickly to heal wounding and improve dynamics in couples relationships.

Barstow, C. (2007). *Right use of power: The heart of ethics.* Boulder, CO: Many Realms Publishing.

This book will take you through the many aspects of power and how to use it in your life and in your practice, if you are a therapist. Cedar Barstow is a long-time Hakomi trainer and applies the theory and practice of Hakomi in this book and explains that not to use your power can be just as detrimental as overusing it.

Ogdon, P. Minton, K., & Pain, C. (2006). *Trauma and the body: A sensorimotor approach to psychotherapy.* New York, NY: W. W. Norton & Company.

This is a truly valuable book on trauma and introduces the sensorimotor approach developed by Pat Odgen. The book includes a chapter on how Hakomi can be used with this approach. Pat Ogden is trained in Hakomi.

Kurtz, R. S., & Prestera, H. (1976). *The body reveals: An illustrated guide to the psychology of the body*. New York, NY: Harper and Row.

This book shows us how the body holds emotions, past experience, and ways of being. It includes valuable insights on what wounding is held and how to work with it. A must for anyone working with the body or even in psychotherapy.

Websites

Hakomi Educational Network
<www.hakomiway.ca> and www.hakominework.org

The Hakomi Institute USA
<www.hakomiinstitute.com>

Emotional Freedom Technique

The Method

Gary Craig, who studied Thought Field Therapy (TFT) with Dr. Roger Callaghan, created the method by simplifying and refining what he had learned so it could be easily applied to any difficulty.

This very simple and rapid technique is used to reduce or eliminate fears and phobias, trapped emotions, and physical symptoms and has many other applications. The method utilizes affirmations and tapping on points located on the acupuncture meridians.

On his original web site <www.emofree.com> Gary wrote "Based on impressive new discoveries involving the body's subtle energies, Emotional Freedom Technique (EFT) has been clinically effective in thousands of cases for trauma and PSTD; stress and anxiety; fears and phobias; depression; addictive cravings; children's issues; and hundreds of physical symptoms, including headaches, body pains, and breathing difficulties.

When properly applied, over 80% of the people using EFT achieve either noticeable improvement or complete cessation of the problem. In addition, this technique:

- Often works where no other technique will;
- Is usually rapid, long lasting, and gentle;
- Does not involve drugs or equipment;
- Is easily learned by anyone;
- Can be self applied. "

EFT is now widely used and acknowledged by health and helping professionals, such as doctors, teachers, coaches, therapists, psychologists, and many others. While the USA body of psychologists does not yet endorse it, there is much research that is being done to support its eventual recognition.

Gary Craig retired in 2011, after so generously offering training and resource material in the method at very little cost through the many DVDs and seminars that he prepared and delivered.

Gary Craig: Founder

Since he officially retired in 2011, Gary Craig has created a new website <www.emofree.com>

Gary Craig has a free EFT tutorial available at www.emofree.com/eft/overview.html Gary has also created tutorials on the Art of Delivery in which he demonstrates and comments on key points of the method and its art of delivery so the practitioner can be more effective.

EFT Universe

EFT Universe was created just before or shortly after Gary's retirement by followers and passionate practitioners of the method in order to promote EFT and provide certificate training. The website is www.eftuniverse.com. You can download the EFT manual for free and rent videos at this website.

To watch a video on EFT by EFT Universe, go to <youtube/9jTNHHTxG40>.

To rent training DVDs, go to <www.1shoppingcart.com/app/?Clk=4757161>.

Certification trainings from EFT Universe are available at <www.1shoppingcart.com/app/?Clk=4757193>.

How I integrate this method into my approach

I find EFT very effective and rapid and I often get surprising results, so much so that I teach basic EFT to almost all my clients and use it in most of my sessions. When well learned and applied, EFT can be very powerful, rapid, and transformative.

EFT has been one of the keys to discovering, trusting, developing, and following my intuition when I am with a client. This has allowed me to move from doing the technique to the art of delivering it.

To my surprise, I have found by doing chakra readings before and after using EFT that the tapping on the meridians points actually has the effect of opening some chakras.

Books

Gary has many very well written and useful books available on different applications of the method. I have read and especially like:

Craig, G. (2008a). *The EFT manual*. Santa Rosa, CA: Energy Psychology Press.

Craig, G. (2008b). *EFT for PTSD (post-traumatic stress disorder)*. Fulton, CA: Energy Psychology Press.

Craig, G. (2010). *EFT for weight loss*. Fulton, CA: Energy Psychology Press.

Websites

Gary Craig <www.emofree.com>

EFT Universe <www.eftuniverse.com>

Internal Family Systems (IFS)

<u>The Method</u>

In IFS, Richard Schwartz introduces a brilliant way of working with all the parts that we have inside us that take on one of three principle roles, many or most of which are unconscious:

- Managers: these parts manage our life experience, usually with a benevolent intent of protecting us from something "bad."

- Firefighters: these parts come in as firefighters when we face a situation that in the past may have been traumatic and that urgently demands a survival reaction.

- Exiles: the parts of ourselves that we have not been able to let live for fear of being ridiculed or hurt.

Schwartz introduces the Essential Self, that part of us that knows very well how to manage our lives and will do it once we tap into its existence and allow its inner knowing, wisdom, and intuition to contribute and take the initiative.

IFS is extremely useful and efficient in bringing awareness to these various parts and transforming them into allies so that their innate wisdom is not lost, but rather is harnessed to enrich the life experience. This frees up the slave and victim of these parts that were created at an early age as survival and coping mechanisms.

New possibilities then emerge to create a nourishing life from the Essential Self.

How I integrate this method into my approach

I discovered Richard Schwartz's (1995) book on internal family systems while studying Hakomi in Prince Edward Island when Hakomi Trainer Greg Johanson brought some of his extensive library to share with us.

I was so taken by what I was reading that I read half the book in one evening and completely caught on to what Richard was putting forth. I immediately integrated the concepts into my work with my clients, especially when it was evident that a part of consciousness was taking over and controlling a particular client's experience.

It has now become one of the key methods in my approach and blends seamlessly with Hakomi and EFT.

Books

Schwartz, R. C. (1995). *Internal family systems therapy*. New York, NY: The Guilford Press.

Schwartz, R. C. (2008). *You are the one you've been waiting for: Bringing courageous love to intimate relationships*. Eugene, OR: Trailheads.

Websites

Internal Family Systems - The Center for Self Leadership

ThetaHealing

The Method

ThetaHealing was created by Vianna Stibal while she healed herself of a cancerous tumor.

The method works directly with the Creator, God, or Source to command healing and then witness the changes that are happening.

It can be used for many things, including DNA activation and working with beliefs, memories, and trauma.

While simple to use, it can be a powerful method for healing.

How I integrate this method into my approach

I mainly use ThetaHealing to activate the latent strands of DNA to release the potential of the client's original blueprint and be a catalyst for developing that full potential.

I occasionally use the other aspects of the method when called for in the work.

Books

Stibal, V. (2000). *Go up and work with God.* Roberts, ID: Rolling Thunder Publishing.

Stibal, V. (2006). *Theta healing.* Idaho Falls, ID: Rolling Thunder Publishing.

Websites

ThetaHealing <www.thetahealing.com>

The Use of Sound in Healing

The Method

You probably have already experienced how different kinds of music can alter your moods and soothe and relax or energize your state. I'm sure you have felt the vibrations from powerful speakers when listening to a band play blues or rock and roll. It has probably moved you to get up and dance.

Sound is vibration, and the physical body mass is really energy as Einstein's formula of relativity $E=MC^2$ demonstrates. The cells, which are made up of molecules comprised of atoms, protons, and electrons, will respond to vibration and this vibration will help to release stuck energy, in the same way that ultrasound is used to disintegrate kidney stones.

Barbara Brennan gives the note for each chakra in *Light Emerging* (Brennan 1993, p. 112). Jonathan Goldman gives the vowel sound associated with each chakra in his book *Healing Sounds: The Power of Harmonic.* (Goldman 1996, p. 118)

Chakra	Music Note (Brennan)	VowelSound (Goldman)
7th chakra – Crown	G	EEE
6th chakra – 3rd Eye	D	AYE
5th chakra – Throat	A	EYE
4th chakra – Heart	G	AH
3rd chakra – Solar Plexus	F	OH
2nd chakra – Sacral	D	OOO
1st chakra - Root	G (below middle C)	UH

It is actually possible to produce more than one vibration at a time with the voice by combining the shape of the mouth with the placement of the tongue and holding the nasal cavities in certain ways. This produces harmonics, which are very effective in healing.

Tibetan Monks are renown for the capacity to tone at really low levels with their voice, as can be heard on many recordings. The sounds they produce help to ground. The "OM" meditation is another powerful use of sound to alter the state of consciousness and align the chakras.

Various healing modalities use different combinations of the vibrations produced by tuning forks, Tibetan bowls, crystal bowls, and voice to remove stuck energy, held emotions, and muscle tensions.

<u>How I integrate this into my approach</u>

I first learned about the impact of sound on the physical body at the Barbara Brennan School of Healing when I saw a movie by Dr. Guy Manners showing sand particles being formed into 3D shapes by sound waves. Barbara also used sound in her healing demonstrations.

After reading Jonathan Goldman's (1996) book on sound healing, I began to experiment with it, and I now incorporate it regularly into my energy work, particularly by using the voice harmonics on each chakra as I lay hands on them. I also use sound on any other areas of the body that calls for it. It feels weird at first to some clients and often brings on uncontrollable laughter, but it is effective in influencing the chakras and other energy blocks.

234

<u>Books</u>

Goldman, J. (1996). *Healing sounds: The power of harmonics*. Boston, MA: Element Books.

Kenyon, T. (1994). *Brain states*. United States Publishing.

<u>Websites</u>

Healing Sounds, Jonathan Goldman
<www.healingsounds.com>

Tom Kenyon, Sound Healer <www.tomkenyon.com>

Core Energetics

The Method

The aim of Core Energetics is to allow the client's core essence to be freely expressed to create joy and pleasure instead of pain and suffering. The work in Core Energetics is to transform and overcome the obstacles that prevent the client from experiencing his or her core.

Core Energetics was created by John Pierrakos, who had previously developed BioEnergetics with Alexander Lowen. Both were students of Wilhelm Reich, who was a student of Freud.

John Pierrakos blended the principles and techniques of BioEnergetics and the spiritual dimensions of the Pathwork of Personal Transformation (see description of the Pathwork in this appendix). Core Energetics is the only body therapy of which I am aware that incorporates the work of consciousness using the spiritual aspects of the Higher Self, Lower Self, and Mask Self.

In Core Energetics, we work with the body to release blocked energy held in the body armor, those places where stuck energy is accumulated and held as tension and muscle spasms. We help the client to become conscious of the spiritual aspects and how they impact his or her reality and get in the way of experiencing joy and pleasure in life.

How I integrate this method into my approach

Barbara Brennan, herself a Core Energetics Therapist, incorporated a lot of development and process work aspects of Core Energetics into the school curriculum at the Barbara Brennan School of Healing. I am inspired by many of the body and consciousness aspects of Core Energetics from my training with Barbara and incorporate them into my work with clients when needed.

Once I complete my training as a Core Therapist over the next two years, I will apply the method directly when appropriate for the client.

Books

Pierrakos, J C. (1990). *Core energetics.* Mendocino, CA: Life Rhythm.

Websites

Institute of Core Energetics <www.coreenergetics.org>

Core Energetics Montreal <www.coreenergeticsmontreal.ca>

Somatic-Psychoeducation (fasciatherapy - Danis Bois Method)

The Method

Danis Bois is a physiotherapist and osteopath who discovered an innate internal movement in the body independent of any other body movement, pulsing at a steady rhythm of two cycles per minute or 15 seconds per travel direction. This movement, coined Sensory Biorhythm, becomes disrupted or ceases altogether when a part of the body suffers trauma or injury and loses sensitivity, perceptibility, and mobility. Essentially, the person has lost connection with him or herself.

Danis explored this movement at length and developed a method to bring the client back into connection with him or herself by treating the fascia, the fine membrane that covers the muscle and organ tissue and holds the memory of all traumas experienced by the body.

The practitioner, with deep presence and slow intentional directional impulses, induces very slow movements and interruptions to the various parts of the body, which restores the body biorhythm and coherence of the different body parts.

The result is a re-education of the body systems to regain sensitivity, mobility, and ability to perceive them. It has a profound impact on the connection to the self. The client regains contact with the different body parts; becomes conscious of where (and perhaps why) there has been disconnection; and, with the help of the therapist's guidance, can begin to apply what comes up to help create new possibilities in his or her life.

The method uses the following five tools:

- Sensory Introspection: meditation centered on the body
- Manual Therapy
- Sensory Movement
- Dialogue
- Writing

How I integrate this method into my approach

I use this method whenever I need to work physically on the body, in addition to working energetically.

Books

Many books exist in French, but I am aware of only one that has been translated into English.

Bois, D. (2009). *The wild region of lived experience: Using somatic psychoeducation.* Berkeley, CA: North Atlantic Books.

Bois, D. Josso, M. C. & Humpich, M. (2009). *Sujet sensible et renouvellement du moi: les contributions de la fasciathérapie et de la somato-psychopédagogie.* Ivry: Point d'appui.

Websites

Center for Applied Research and Study
<www.cerap.org/index.php/en>

Yoga

Yoga originated in India as a way to prepare the body for deep meditation practices. The word originates from a Sanskrit work that means "yoke," or to join—joining body and mind or spirit. Yoga practice unifies the body and the mind, increases muscle strength and flexibility, relaxes, increases the power of the breath, and has many healing effects on physical and psychological levels.

I have found that doing fifteen to thirty minutes of yoga on a daily basis for the last thirty years or so has helped me to keep my muscles toned as well as improve and maintain flexibility.

In addition, my breathing and aerobic capacity seem to be above average; I especially notice this when I am doing sports and physical exercise in the company of others, who often seem to be out of breath with relatively little effort while my breath remains slow and regular.

There are many different kinds of yoga, too numerous to mention, each with its own focus.

Yoga studios abound and are easily accessible; the courses are relatively inexpensive.

The great thing about a Yoga practice is that you can do it at home or wherever you happen to be. You can take it with you.

Meditation

The English word meditation is derived from the Latin word "meditatio", which means "to think, contemplate, or ponder."

The many forms of meditation aim to train the mind to avoid being taken over by extraneous thoughts and to develop an ability to be mindful and aware. Meditation practice develops the Observing Self, so that the Observer becomes detached from the part that is experiencing. This enhances the ability to focus and lessens the drama around experience. A person who meditates regularly is more relaxed, self-aware, and better able to respond to experience. Through consistent practice, one eventually becomes more detached from the Ego or the "I" with which one usually completely identifies.

Ultimately, the goal is to develop the ability to be in continuous meditation or continually aware and to live life with the Observer always active and observing what the Self is experiencing.

Yogis and Tibetan monks in deep states of meditation can control their body and brain functions. Many studies have recently been done using brain scans that confirm the effect of meditation on brain activity and function. Several of these are quoted in *The Mindful Brain* (Siegel, 2007).

There are many forms of meditation, some very passive and some very active. Meditation can be done in the classic cross-legged sitting position or while eating, walking, or engaging in other kinds of movement. Some forms of meditation include:

- Transcendental Meditation, which became very popular in the last part of the 20th century and is still widely practiced. Many scientific experiments have been done, as can be found on the website: www.trancenet.org/tmresearch.htm. Some research has shown that in cities where a large number of people did this type of meditation at the same time, the crime rate actually dropped.

- Mindfulness Meditation, which is widely promoted by Thich Nhât Hanh and develops the capacity to be mindfully aware.

- Vipassana Meditation, a form of meditation taught by Buddha that can be experienced in 3- and 10-day intensives.

- Zen Meditation, which is well known and widely practiced.

Meditation can be practiced alone or in a group. The collective energy of a group will reinforce and deepen the experience of meditation.

You don't necessarily need to meditate for hours for it to be beneficial. Simply sitting for ten to fifteen minutes a day can help to center and calm the mind.

Ratu Bagus Shaking Meditation

I experienced this bio-energetic meditation during a six-day stay at the Ratu Bagus Ashram in Bali, Indonesia, and I found it so effective that I continue to practice it every day.

A spiritual teacher with extraordinary powers, Ratu Bagus developed a form of bio-energy meditation, training local and international students in his center (the Ratu Bagus Ashram) on the slopes of Mount Agung in Bali, Indonesia.

The following text is reproduced, with permission, from the website www.ratubagus.com.

To some it's known as Shaking, a truly life-changing practice, made possible by the transmission that comes from the energy master Ratu Bagus. This energy transmission ignites the sacred fire that lies dormant within each of us and calls upon our own energy system, to remember and "wake up" the natural capacity our bodies have for healing, on the physical, emotional, mental and spiritual levels.

This energy is complete as it works on many levels, not just the physical, with an emphasis on "practice", rather than theory or technique. Ratu teaches us that greater understanding of ourselves happens not with the mind but when we allow the energy to connect with a much deeper part of ourselves—through our own experience. Then transformation is allowed to happen spontaneously, removing all blocks that prevent us from achieving our highest potential.

The Practice

The practice manifests as movement of the body. Following the very high vibration of the energy, we may feel the body shaking or spontaneously moving or spinning which is both simple and powerful. Many practitioners report life-changing results in a very short space of time.

When we tune into the connection with the energy, the body "remembers" and the energy then begins to move us. This feels amazing; some describe it as feeling like heat in the body or a feeling of electricity or fire inside. Others say it feels like connecting with their soul, the God inside, their original self.

When we practice, we allow the energy into our bodies and trust that this intelligent energy will give us everything we need. This sacred fire will return us to our natural state of harmony, unity, peace, joy and radiant health. This gift is there for everyone, there's no age or ability that can't practice Bio Energy Meditation.

"Om Swastiastu Ratu Bagus"

This mantra is used throughout the practice, while meditating and while training. By focusing our attention on it we are calling to the energy to help us. Ratu says it's very simple, but complete.

The Process

Processing is fundamental to growth in the practice. As the energy becomes stronger in the body, it pushes out anything which is negative. This processing is the body's natural way of cleansing itself. This physical and emotional release can manifest in many ways, such as coughing, laughing, shouting, dancing, etc.

The more we practice and build a relationship with the divine light within, the more it can teach us. The answers to the deep questions we have about ourselves, our life and our purpose become clear. Over time, life regains its magical quality, we feel a greater ability to connect with life, become healthier, more vibrant and feel a greater sense of freedom and love for ourselves and those around us.

<u>Laughing Medicine</u>

Central to Ratu's teaching is to be positive; to live from that energy no matter what is happening in our lives. During the training people often experience uncontrollable laughter, real laughter that comes from deep within, from the soul. Ratu says that when we experience this laughter it wakes up all the chakras, enabling the energy to work very well in the body. Laughing helps the connection with the soul, then it's easy to take care of the physical body, with this strong connection with the divine we can become free. We can release all attachments, raise our consciousness and find paradise inside by following our laughter. Ratu always says "Problem—No Problem", when we laugh we allow life to become full of positive thinking and feeling.

"When we practice we learn to love ourselves and then we can go through life with a smile. Loving ourselves means that we are healing ourselves" - Ratu Bagus

<u>Books</u>

Donder, K. (n.d.) *Ratu Bagus Bio-Energy*. Muncan, Bali, Indonesia: Ratu Bagus Ashram.

This book is only available through the Ratu Bagus Ashram website at the moment.

Another book, written in Indonesian, is in the process of being translated into English.

<u>Websites</u>

Ratu Bagus Ashram <www.ratubagus.com>

Biodanza

It is difficult to explain Biodanza; participating is really the best way to experience it. During the six years that I have been practicing on a weekly basis, I can say that it has helped me to deepen my ability to relate to others. I am more comfortable in a group. I have grown in self-love and self-confidence and am more grounded in my identity, and all this transpires in my relationships. I have also developed wonderful friendships.

I am not a qualified facilitator, but let me try to describe it for you from my experience.

Biodanza is a group activity that is designed to evoke a present moment experience of life in all its intensity, completely felt and fully experienced in the moment. In other words it fosters "a total experience of life, a feeling of being intensely alive." This "event" is called a Vivencia, a term coined by its creator Rolando Toro. It is an affectivo-motor system that integrates what is going on inside of us with our bodies and vice versa.

Vivencias always start with a sharing circle in which participants talk about their experience of previous vivencias and how it affected them, unless, of course, they are totally new to it. After this, the facilitator introduces and elaborates on the theme of the evening (or the day or weekend, whatever the case may be). The vivencia begins and ends with a circle dance. Throughout, the facilitator proposes various exercises to be done alone, with a partner, or in a group. The facilitator then demonstrates the exercise to stimulate the participants and their mirror neurons, after which the participants are invited to do the exercise. All exercises are done without words.

Regular participants benefit from a deepening of the process and relationships between group members.

246

Biodanza focuses on, and is supportive of, what is going well to help improve, without any focused effort, what might be difficult in life. In that sense, it is a transformative process.

For newcomers, it is possible to live the experience during introductory evenings or by joining a weekly group.

<u>Website</u>

Biodanza www.biodanza.org

Other Effective Approaches

The Pathwork

Eva Brock channeled the spiritual consciousness of "The Guide" that is transcribed in a series of 258 lectures. This series of channelings became the foundation for the Pathwork, a four-year path of spiritual awakening and transformation.

The following excerpt about the Pathwork® is used with permission from the International Pathwork Foundation. For more information about the Pathwork, please visit www.pathwork.org.

The Pathwork is a spiritual path of self-purification and self-transformation on all levels of consciousness. It emphasizes the importance of recognizing, accepting, learning to know and ultimately transforming our Lower Self or shadow side of our nature. Pathwork helps us understand that through honest self-examination, with carefully applied tools and practices, we can overcome and remove the inner obstacles that keep us from living fully from and in our Godself, our true nature.

We all yearn for deeper, more loving relationships, and we all want more physical pleasure, vitality, and abundance. Ultimately, we want a sense of purpose for our lives that only comes with intimate contact with God. The Pathwork is a collection of teachings that helps us see and understand ourselves, enabling us to gradually remove the obstacles that keep us separate from others, separate from the source of our creativity and life energy, from our divine core.

The Pathwork is not dogmatic. It has no required belief system and does not ask that we abandon religious practices or beliefs that nurture and support us. It does ask us to be willing to examine our beliefs, and to accept the ultimate authority of the true Self. Pathwork also encourages us to develop a healthy, mature ego. For it is only when the ego is strengthened, and purified of its misconceptions about life and its own task, that it can look beyond itself and recognize that it is only a part-albeit a vital part-of our greater self. By using the ego to transcend itself, we are afforded a way to become fully and consciously who we are: our Real Self, our Godself.

Books

Pierrakos, E. (1990). *The pathwork of self-transformation.* Del Mar, CA: Pathwork Press.

Thesenga, S. (1994). *The undefended self.* Del Mar, CA: Pathwork Press.

Pierrakos, E, compiled by Saly, J. (1993). *Creating union: A compilation of Eva's lectures.* Del Mar, CA: Pathwork Press.

Thesenga, D. (1993). *Fear no evil: The Pathwork Method of transforming the lower self.* Del Mar, CA: Pathwork Press.

Website

Pathwork Foundation <www.pathwork.org>

Byron Katie's The Work

The Method

Byron Katie has developed a remarkably simple and effective way of looking at the difficulties we have in life and accepting reality as it is rather than how we would like it to be.

The technique involves asking four short questions about the situation that we are unhappy with and is triggering us, and then turning it around to allow us to look at other aspects.

After identifying what the difficulty is, as in "John bullies me," the four questions to ask are?" (Katie, 2002, p. 15):

- Is it true?

- Can you absolutely know that it's true?

- How do you react when you think that thought?

- Who would you be without the thought

Then you turn it around—say it another way. For example, if your difficulty is "John bullies me" then you explore turning it around in various ways like:

- I bully John or,

- I bully others

Byron has created a school to train in the method and organizes intensives in which participants can learn and work on their challenges and transform their experience of reality.

She has trained many therapists to assist people in the process.

Books

Katie, B. (2002). *Loving what is: Four questions that can change your life.* New York, NY: Harmony Books.

Website

The Work <www.thework.com>

Nonviolent Communication

Nonviolent communication was created by Marshall Rosenberg.

In *Nonviolent Communication*, (Rosenberg, 1999) the author first shows us that communication, in the way it is most often done, blocks compassion. He then demonstrates how to observe without evaluating or judging and also how to recognize our feelings and emotions. He makes the distinction between feelings and non-feelings. And he then talks about taking responsibility.

He explains that anger is a signal that a need has not been met, and he shows how to identify that need. He teaches his method of communicating from our truth without blaming ourselves or the other, talking about the facts observed, expressing anger, and making a request (not a demand) in order to prevent the situation from repeating itself."

This very efficient method is taught worldwide. You can join a practice circle to integrate the method into daily life.

Books

Rosenberg, M. (2003). *Non-violent communication.* Encinitas, CA: PuddleDancer Press.

D'Ansembourg, T. (2010). *Cessez d'être gentil: soyez vrai !.* Montréal: les Éd. de l'homme.

Vidal-Graf, S., & Vidal-Graf, C. (2002). *La colère, cette émotion mal aimée: exprimer sa colère sans violence.* Saint-Julien-en-Genevois: Jouvence.

<u>Website</u>

The Center for Nonviolent Communication

Ho O'ponopono

In *Zero Limits* (Vitale, 2007) the author relates that Dr. Ihaleakala Hew Len used this method to completely close a wing of a psychiatric hospital by healing all the patients without working directly with them.

The method is based on taking total responsibility for everyone's actions (not only your own). The application of the method is deceptively simple—it involves repeating these four short phrases while holding the situation or problem in your consciousness "I love you. I'm sorry. Please forgive me. Thank you."

According to Dr. Len, the difficulty in our lives is caused by replaying old memories that are stored in our consciousness (ours or those we share with others). These phrases work to clean the memories and release them, and this allows us to create what we really want in our lives from the newly created "Zero State," a state of infinite, unrealized possibilities.

Books

Vitale, J. & Hew Len, I. (2007). *Zero Limits*. Hoboken, NJ: John Wiley & Sons.

Websites

Ho'oponopono – Resources and Tools
<www.ho-oponopono.org>

The Practice of Tonglen

Tonglen is a practice of compassion, the core of which is breathing in our own, or someone else's, suffering and breathing out compassion or healing emotions related to the specific suffering being addressed.

It is unifying in that when doing Tonglen, we realize that our suffering, or the suffering of someone else, is in fact being experienced by many other people at the same time. In this way, by working on ourselves or on a particular situation, we are helping to heal all others.

Tonglen can be practiced as a formal meditation or at any moment when it feels needed and appropriate.

Soygal Rinpoche devotes a complete chapter to the practice in *The Tibetan Book of Living and Dying* (Rinpoche, 1993, ch. 12) *explaining* the steps of how to do it for ourselves, others, or the environment.

Pema Chodron has a very complete and concise description of the practice on her website referenced below.

Books

Rinpoche, S. (1993). *The Tibetan book of living and dying.* New York, NY: Harper Collins.

Chodron, P. (1997). *When things fall apart: Heart advice for difficult times.* Boston, MA: Shambala Publications.

Website

Shambala, Pema Chodron
<www.shambhala.org/teachers/pema/tonglen1.php>

BIBLIOGRAPHY

Bach, R. (1977). *Illusions: The reflections of a reluctant messiah*. New York, NY: Dell Publishing.

Barstow, C. (2007). *Right use of power: The heart of ethics*. Boulder, CO: Many Realms Publishing.

Bois, D. (2009). *The wild region of lived experience: Using somatic psychoeducation*. Berkeley, CA: North Atlantic Books.

Bois, D., Josso, M. C., & Humpich, M. (2009). *Sujet sensible et renouvellement du moi: les contributions de la fasciathérapie et de la somato-psychopédagogie. Ivry: Point d'appui.*

Brennan, B. A. (1993). *Light emerging*. New York, NY: Bantam Books.

Brennan, B. A. (1988). *Hands of light*. New York, NY: Bantam Books.

Brennan, B. (1999). *Seeds of the spirit*. Barbara Brennan Inc.

Chodron, P. (1997). *When things fall apart: Heart advice for difficult times*. Boston, MA: Shambala Publications.

Craig, G. (2008a). *The EFT manual*. Santa Rosa, CA: Energy Psychology Press.

Craig, G. (2008b). *EFT for PTSD (post-traumatic stress disorder)*. Fulton, CA: Energy Psychology Press.

Craig, Gary. (2010). *EFT for weight loss*. Fulton, CA: Energy Psychology Press.

D'Ansembourg, T. (2010). *Cessez d'être gentil : soyez vrai !*. Montréal : les Éd. de l'homme.

Dale, C. (2009). *The subtle body: An encyclopedia of your energetic anatomy.* Boulder, CO: Sounds True.

Desjardins, A. (1998). *L'audace de vivre.* Paris: La Table Ronde.

Desjardins, A. (2002). *Arnaud Desjardins au Québec.* Montréal: Stanké.

Donder, K. (n.d.) *Ratu Bagus Bio-Energy.* Muncan, Bali, Indonesia: Ratu Bagus Ashram.

Fisher, R. (2002). *Experiential psychotherapy with couples: A guide for the creative pragmatist.* Phoenix, AZ: Zeig, Tucker and Theisen Inc.

Ford, D. (1998). *The dark side of the light chasers.* New York, NY: Riverhead Books.

Frost, R. (1916). *Mountain interval.* New York, NY: Henry Holt and Company.

Goldman, J. (1996). *Healing sounds: The power of harmonics.* Boston, MA: Element Books.

Grad, B. R. (1965). Some biological effects of laying-on of hands: A review of experiments with animals and plants. *Journal of the American Society for Psychical Research, 59,* 95-127.

Haberly, H. J. (1990). *Hawayo Takata's story.* Olney, MD: Archedigm Publications.

Honervogt, T. (1998). *The power of Reiki: An ancient hands-on healing technique.* New York, NY: Owl Books - Henry Holt and Company.

Horan, P. (1990). *Empowerment through Reiki: The path to personal and global transformation.* Twin Lakes, WI: Lotus Light Publications.

Horan, P. (1995). *Abundance through Reiki*. Twin Lakes, WI: Lotus Light Publications.

Johanson, G., & Kurtz, R. S. (1991). *Grace unfolding: Psychotherapy in the spirit of the Tao-te Ching*. New York, NY: Bell Tower.

Johnson, S. M. (1985). *Characterological transformation*: *The hard work miracle*. Markham, ON: Penguin Books.

Johnson, S. M. (1994). *Character styles*. New York, NY: W. W. Norton & Company.

Judith, A. & S. Vega (1993). *The sevenfold journey: Reclaiming mind, body, and spirit through chakras*. Freedom, CA: Crossing Press.

Judith, A. (2004). *Eastern body, Western mind*. Berkeley, CA: Celestial Arts.

Katie, B. (2002). *Loving what is*: *Four questions that can change your life*. New York, NY: Harmony Books.

Kenyon, T. (1994). *Brain states*. United States Publishing.

Kornfield, J. (1993). *A path with heart: A guide through the perils and promises of spiritual life*. New York: Bantam Books.

Kurtz, R. S., & Prestera, H. (1976). *The body reveals: An illustrated guide to the psychology of the body*. New York, NY: Harper and Row.

Kurtz, R. S. (1990). *Body-centered psychotherapy: The Hakomi Method*. Mondocino, CA: LifeRhythm.

Lowen, A. (1995). *Joy: The surrender to the body and to life*. New York, NY: Penguin Books.

Lübeck, W. (1996). *Way of the heart.* Twin Lakes, WI: Lotus Press.

Lübeck, W., Petter, F. A., & Rand, W. L. (2001). *The spirit of Reiki.* Twin Lakes, WI: Lotus Press.

Mary, R. (2005). *Le Reiki aujourd'hui: De l'origine aux pratiques actuelles.* Barret-su-Méouge, FR: Le Souffle d'Or.

Motz, J. (1998). *Hands of life.* New York, NY: Bantam Books.

Ogdon, P., Minton, K., & Pain, C. (2006). *Trauma and the body: A sensorimotor approach to psychotherapy.* New York, NY: W. W. Norton & Company.

Pierrakos, E. (1990). *The pathwork of self-transformation.* Del Mar, CA: Pathwork Press.

Pierrakos, E, compiled by Saly, J. (1993). *Creating union: A compilation of Eva's lectures.* Del Mar, CA: Pathwork Press.

Pierrakos, J. C. (1990). *Core energetics.* Mendocino, CA: Life Rhythm.

Rinpoche, S. (1993). *The Tibetan book of living and dying.* New York, NY: Harper Collins.

Rosenberg, M. (2003). *Non-violent communication.* Encinitas, CA: PuddleDancer Press.

Schwartz, R. C. (1995). *Internal family systems therapy.* New York, NY, The Guilford Press.

Schwartz, R. C. (2008). *You are the one you've been waiting for: Bringing courageous love to intimate relationships.* Eugene, OR: Trailheads.

Siegel, D. J. (2007). *The mindful brain: Reflection and attunement in the cultivation of well-being.* New York, NY: W. W. Norton & Company.

Stibal, V. (2000). *Go up and work with God.* Roberts, ID: Rolling Thunder Publishing.

Stibal, V. (2006). *Thetahealing.* Idaho Falls, ID: Rolling Thunder Publishing.

Taylor, K. (1995). *The ethics of caring: Honoring the web of life in our professional healing relationships.* Santa Cruz, CA: Handford Mead Publishers.

Thesenga, D. (1993). *Fear no evil: The Pathwork Method of transforming the lower self.* Del Mar, CA: Pathwork Press.

Thesenga, S. (1994). *The undefended self.* Del Mar, CA: Pathwork Press.

Tolle, E. (2004). *The power of now: A guide to spiritual enlightenment.* Novato, CA: New World Library.

Tolle, E. (2005). *A new earth: Awakening to your life's purpose.* Detroit, MI: Gale.

Vidal-Graf, S. & Vidal-Graf, C. (2002). *La colère, cette émotion mal aimée : exprimer sa colère sans violence.* Saint-Julien-en-Genevois : Jouvence.

Vitale, J, & Hew Len, I. (2007). *Zero limits: The secret Hawaiian system for wealth.* Hoboken, NJ: John Wiley and Sons.

Williamson, M. (1992). *A return to love: Reflections on the principles of a Course in Miracles.* New York: Harper Collins.

ABOUT THE AUTHOR

Roland has been a Reiki Master since 1997 and has been teaching Reiki since 1998.

After having worked for 28 years in the field of engineering as an engineer and project manager, he changed the course of his life to become a healing facilitator in order to work closely with individuals to accompany them on their personal journey of healing and transformation.

Since he graduated from the Barbara Brennan School of Healing in 2002, he has continued to study and add tools to integrate into his global approach.

He has completed the advanced studies in education at the Barbara Brennan School of Healing, is a certified Hakomi practitioner and trainer, holds basic and advanced certificates in EFT, as well as a certificate in Somato-PsychoEducation (SPE) and fasciatherapy (Danis Bois Method). He is currently training in Core Energetics.

Roland works with individuals and offers Reiki courses as well as various other workshops in personal growth and transformation.

He currently practices in Montreal, Quebec, Canada.

OTHER WORKS BY THE AUTHOR

Digital English edition of this book

A digital (eBook) version of this book is available on the following web sites:

Reiki – A Powerful Catalyst for Personal Growth and Healing

ISBN-13: 978-0-9919112-1-9

<www.smashwords.com/books/view/301876>

<www.amazon.com>

French versions of this book

French digital (eBook) and print versions are available on the following web sites:

Digital edition

Le Reiki – Puissant catalyseur de transformation personnelle et de guérison

ISBN-13: 978-0-9919112-0-2

<www.smashwords.com/books/view/303114>

<www.amazon.com>

Print edition

Le Reiki – Puissant catalyseur de transformation personnelle et de guérison

ISBN-13: 978-0-9919112-3-3

Articles

The following articles by the author are available on this web page:

<www.rolandberard.com/Production/EN/MyArticles.htm>

- Charting the Progress of Healing using Brennan Healing Science – An Evaluation of Results
- The Power of Intention in Focusing Groups
- Reiki and Brennan Healing Science— Similarities and Differences

CPSIA information can be obtained at www.ICGtesting.com
Printed in the USA
LVOW01s1956020714

392722LV00043B/1939/P